Sullivan County Recollections

By
Henry Harrison Metcalf

Revised and Republished from
The Argus-Champion

HERITAGE BOOKS
2025

HERITAGE BOOKS
AN IMPRINT OF HERITAGE BOOKS, INC.

Books, CDs, and more—Worldwide

For our listing of thousands of titles see our website
at
www.HeritageBooks.com

A Facsimile Reprint
Published 2025 by
HERITAGE BOOKS, INC.
Publishing Division
5810 Ruatan Street
Berwyn Heights, MD 20740

The Argus Press
Newport, New Hampshire
1926

— Publisher's Notice —
In reprints such as this, it is often not possible to remove
blemishes from the original. We feel the contents of this
book warrant its reissue despite these blemishes and
hope you will agree and read it with pleasure.

International Standard Book Number
Paperbound: 978-0-7884-2725-1

Sullivan County Recollections

I first saw the light of day, as I have been credibly informed, though I have no distinct recollection of the fact, on the seventh day of April, 1841, in a small three room cottage, in the northwest part of the town of Newport, near the point where the towns of Newport, Claremont, Cornish and Croydon come together. Here was my home for the first five years of my life, and in this school district, which was a union district, including the northwest section of Newport and a small portion of the southwest section of Croydon, I attended my first two terms of school.

Among the more prominent families in this district were the Metcalf and Ward families in the Croydon section, and the Chapins, Goulds, and Fletchers in Newport, though another family of Metcalfs had also been reared in the Newport portion. The head of the Metcalf family of Croydon, at the time of my birth, was Moses Metcalf, who had succeeded his father, Captain Obed Metcalf, as proprietor of the farm which the latter had cleared up from the wilderness in which he had settled shortly after the close of the Revolution, coming up from Franklin, Mass., (formerly West Wrentham) where he was born.

He was a son of Lieut. Samuel Metcalf, a soldier of the Revolution, who fought at Bunker Hill and, under various enlistments, throughout the war. Other sons of Lieut. Samuel Metcalf were Abel and Samuel, the former settling in Newport and the latter in another part of Croydon. With these sons, it may be added, the old soldier spent his declining years, and his remains have long reposed in a Croydon cemetery.

Capt. Obed Metcalf (my grandfather) was prominent in town and church affairs, serving many years as a selectman, and twice as a Representative in the General Court. He was a member of the committee that built the Congregational Church at the "Four Corners," over a hundred years ago, and for a long time commanded the Croydon company in the old state militia; hence his title of Captain. He had six children—three sons and three daughters. Of his sons Moses was the eldest, Joseph P. (my father) second, and Stephen, who was for many years a prominent citizen of the town of Haverhill, the youngest.

As I recall it, Moses Metcalf, with whom my grandmother remained, on the old homestead after my grandfather's decease, had a family of eight children—four sons and four daughters. Of the daughters the eldest died in youth; the others, with the exception of the youngest, married and went West, while Ursula, the youngest, who was the only one whom I ever knew, remained at home, except when occasionally engaged as a teacher. The eldest son, Cyrenus, went to California when the gold fever first broke out, but did not remain long. Returning he learned the stone cutter's trade, and located in Minnesota, but soon went farther west, where he ultimately died. The second son, Obed, went West later, while the two younger sons, Williams and Edwin (the latter about my age) remained at home.

The Ward place was in possession of Alfred Ward, a thrifty farmer, who had inherited the same from his father, Josiah Ward, who came from Henniker when a young man and settled here, rearing a family of ten children who grew to maturity and all passed middle life, while two others died young. These were Sally, David, Josiah, Eliza, Thomas, Alfred, Lenora, Daniel, Gilbert, and Livona—four daughters and six sons. David, the eldest son, was a physician and settled in Illinois. Josiah was a lawyer, located for a time in Michigan and afterwards in Illinois, but ultimately in Nevada. Thomas went West early in life and was last heard from in California, where he died in 1866. Daniel, like David, became a physician and practiced in the same state; while Gilbert, the youngest son was a farmer and settled not far from home. Alfred Ward, who married Randilla Powers, a member of the noted Croydon family of that name, and was a prominent Croydon citizen, had two daughters—Elizabeth and Ermina. Sally, the oldest daughter of Josiah Ward, married Gideon Gould.

Abel Metcalf, as has been said, settled here, but he had "passed on" and his family all departed before my time. He was a pious and exemplary man, and a deacon of the Baptist Church. He had three sons and a daughter, the latter dying young. Of the sons Silas, the eldest, was a farmer, settled in another section of the town. Theron, the second was engaged in mercantile affairs in Claremont and Boston, while the youngest son, Kendrick, gained a liberal education, graduating from Dartmouth College and entering the Episcopal ministry. He ultimately became a member of the faculty of Hobart College, at Geneva, N. Y., and held the Latin professorship in that institution, for more than forty years, serving at one time as acting President. I met him once, on the occasion of a visit to his native town, when we both happened to be "marooned" in the Newport House, at the time of the great freshet, in the fall of 1869.

Near the Deacon Metcalf place was the home of Deacon Timothy Fletcher, another "pillar" of the Baptist Church, whose wife was Lois Metcalf, daughter of Lieutenant Samuel and a sister of the other Metcalfs mentioned. They had two daughters and four sons. One of the daughters—Aurilla, became the wife of Austin L. Kibbey, a successful farmer living in the northern part of Newport, while the other—Laura, married one Josiah Nichols and lived in Sutton. The eldest son—Samuel M. (generally known by his middle name of Metcalf,) went west in early life, and ultimately settled in Oregon, as did the youngest son, Benjamin. Cyrus K., the second son, (generally known as Kingsbury) became a Croydon farmer, and was long a prominent citizen of that town. He was the father of Melvin Fletcher of that town, and grandfather of Mrs. S. C. Newell, wife of Newport's present postmaster. The third son, Timothy S. or Stillman (as usually called) continued as a Newport resident, was three times married and had quite a family.

Perhaps the best farm in this district was that of Frederick Chapin, whose father, Daniel Chapin, had settled thereon about 1780, and reared a family of twelve children—seven sons and five daughters. Two of the sons became Congregational ministers; while the youngest, Addison, was a physician, but died early, while in practice in the town of Winchester. Another son was David B., who was the Newport village blacksmith for many years and a deacon of the

Congregational church. One of the daughters—Malvina, married a clergyman named George B. Rowell, and went with him as a missionary to the Sandwich Islands, now Hawaii, the first to engage in such enterprise in that region. Frederick Chapin became one of the most enterprising and successful farmers in town, having a superior herd of cattle and other fine stock. He was unfortunate in his family, however, as his two children, both sons, died in early life.

Another fine farm in the district was that settled by Nathan Gould of Hopkinton in the latter part of the 18th century, where he reared a family of four sons and six daughters, the elder son, Gideon, succeeding him as proprietor of the homestead, which became known as "Fruit Farm" under the ownership of his son, Alfred. Most of the children of Nathan Gould migrated west to Michigan, Ohio and western New York, in which latter region one son, (Carlos,) became a prominent Methodist clergyman, and was at one time a presiding elder in the Genessee Conference. One son, Nathan, however, remained in his native town, married a widow Sherman, originally Nancy Wheeler, and lived on a small farm half a mile below his birthplace. One daughter of Nathan, the elder, died in young womanhood, while Lucy, the youngest, married my father, Joseph P. Metcalf.

I have faint recollection of the teacher during my first summer term of school attendance. I merely remember that her name was Caroline Hall, and I have an impression that her father was James Hall of Newport. Of her subsequent history I know nothing.

The teacher of my first winter school, made up of from 30 to 40 scholars of all ages from 4 to 18, was one Ellen Putnam of Croydon, an accomplished young lady, who subsequently settled in Kansas. She was a daughter of John Putnam, a leading citizen of Croydon and an older sister of George F. Putnam, a leading lawyer of Grafton County, active in Democratic politics, who finally removed to Kansas City, where he died some 20 years ago.

I can recall the names of comparatively few of my schoolmates of eighty years ago; but in all probability none of them are now living. The three younger children of my uncle, Moses Metcalf, Williams, Ursula and Edwin, were among them, the latter being about my age. Williams and Ursula subsequently became teachers but all removed to Minnesota, seventy years ago, with their parents, five older children having already made their home in different parts of the country.

Another was Elizabeth, eldest daughter of Alfred Ward, who subsequently married Edmund B. Richardson of Lempster, and died many years ago. Their son, Cleon, married a daughter of George B. Griffith, the Lempster poet, who died a few years later, as he also did about two years ago. The younger daughter, Ermina Ward, who has resided in Concord for many years past, was not then of school age.

Still another was Sarah Melendy, who made her home at Deacon Fletcher's. She later became the wife of Bela Chapin and settled with him in Claremont. He had been a printer, was a great student and a poet of no mean order and finally became a farmer. They both lived to a great old age.

My cousin, Alfred Gould, son of Gideon, who lived on the old Gould homestead, where my mother was born, was a year older than I. He remained at home, carried on the farm with great success and became a prominent citizen of the town, dying about eight years ago.

Others whom I recall, were two Ames boys, Worthen and Jeduthan, sons of Jacob Ames, a Croydon man, who moved on to the Peabody place, so-called, located below the Gould farm toward Northville, which had been originally settled by one Moses Peabody, who reared a large family there. What became of Jeduthan I am unaware, but Worthen, who was three years older than I, was a brilliant scholar, graduated with high honor from Wesleyan University, and entered the Methodist ministry, but died soon after.

Whether the small cottage in which I was born is still standing, or not, I am unable to say. It was located midway between the Gould place, and the corner where the Cornish and Croydon highway intersected and near which the schoolhouse stood. It was some two miles above Northville, from which scattered settlement, which included several small manufacturing establishments, there were two highways leading to Newport village, the northerly one through the village and passing the Austin Corbin place, and the other over the ridge, and by the old Jenks place originally settled by Jeremiah Jenks, who came from Smithfield, R. I., and settled here about 1770. He became the largest land holder in town and reared one of the largest families. His son Oliver succeeded to the homestead, and also became a prominent citizen and reared a large family. Two of his sons settled in Concord and were well known citizens there. George E. was long associated with Asa McFarland in the newspaper business, as publisher of the Republican Statesman, and held the office of State Printer at one time; but suddenly disappeared, and was never after heard from, so far as any one now knows. Edward A. was also later in the newspaper business, as manager of the company publishing the Republican Statesman and Concord Monitor, but passed on a number of years since.

Another descendant of Jeremiah Jenks, born on this place, was Thomas B., who went to Cumberland, R. I., and engaged in cotton manufacturing. He was the father of Thomas A. Jenks, noted congressman and father of the civil service law.

From my birth place and early home, which was about two miles above Northville, as I recollect, the most conspicuous house on the road, below the Gould place was the large, square, two story yellow house, known as the Morse place, where Ichabod Morse kept a hotel in the early days. I recall nothing about this man, Morse, but I remember that he had a daughter who was the wife of Hon. Harvey Huntoon of East Unity, to which place, by the way, my father removed with his family in April 1846, when I was five years of age.

Northville was a scattered hamlet, containing a number of small manufacturing establishments, some located on Morse brook, and some on the Sugar River, wooden rakes and scythes being the principal production. The scythe factory, originally operated by one Sylvester Larned, later by Larned and Sibley, and subsequently by E. T. Sibley and Son, was quite an important industry, and has continued as such down to the present day. Its product went all over New England, and beyond its borders, and I well remember that it was with a Sibley scythe that I learned to mow, back in the days before mowing machines had come into use.

Going down to Newport village from Northville, by the northern or valley route, the most notable place on the route was the Corbin place, home of Hon. Austin Corbin, Sr., who had a large and well kept farm and a fine stock of cattle. Here it was that the three Corbin boys, Austin, Daniel C. and James, who became prominent in various activities, were born. Austin was educated to the law, and was for a time in partnership with the late Governor Ralph Metcalf in Newport, but soon removed to Davenport, Ia., where he engaged in banking and his was the first bank chartered under the National banking law. Subsequently he removed to New York where he established the Corbin Banking Company, built the Long Island railroad, and engaged in various development enterprises. Daniel C., after extensive operations elsewhere in the West, settled in Spokane, Wash., and was a leader in the upbuilding of that now thriving city; while James located at Silver City, New Mexico, of which he was Mayor, and engaged in large real estate operations.

Just below the Corbin place we passed over the North branch of the Sugar river, by a covered bridge. This, to my childish eyes, seemed a big stream. It was the first river I had ever seen, and was about as wonderful, to my mind, as was Croydon Mountain, which loomed up in the view on the return trip from the village, in rugged grandeur, and was the first mountain which my eyes ever rested upon.

Among the objective points in my father's visits to the village, on some of which I was privileged to accompany him, was the grist mill, to which the farmers from all the surrounding region brought their corn and wheat to be ground into meal and flour. Every farmer of any consequence in those days raised wheat as well as corn, from which the flour for family use was produced. This old mill stood where the present grist mill stands, but it is safe to say that little if any wheat flour is now produced there, though wheat culture is coming into vogue again in some sections of the state.

Speaking of mills, it is a matter of history that the first saw and grist mills in Newport were built by Benjamin Giles, one of the first settlers, at the point now known as Guild, who was given a grant of land in consideration of his enterprise. This man, Giles, was prominent in the affairs of the colony, was a delegate in the Provincial Congress, and a member of the committee which drafted the form of independent government, established in January, 1776, the anniversary of which the state has recently celebrated. He was also a member of the Council established under that government.

The first visit to Newport village, of which I have any recollection, was when, at the age of four years, I accompanied my father to a Sunday morning service in the stately old Congregational church at the South end, then as now one of the most imposing church edifices in the state, and which I entered with a feeling of awe, which was in no way dispelled as I looked upon the solemn face and listened to the no less solemn tones of the preacher, as from the lofty pulpit he overlooked the congregation in their old square pews, and warned them of the awful fate awaiting the unbeliever—a message which I failed to comprehend in full, but which seemed to visibly affect some portion of the audience.

This church edifice, which was built in 1822— 104 years ago—was the third house of worship erected in town by the Congregationalists, who predominated among the early settlers and practically controlled the town, the first being a small, rough structure used for church and school purposes, located near what has since been known as the "Claggett Place," on the Unity road, built in 1775, and the second, a more pretentious affair, also on the West side of the river near the foot of "Claremont Hill," completed twenty years later.

This pastor, whose preaching was the first that I ever heard, was the Rev. John Woods, who settled over the church in 1824, coming from Warner where he had previously been settled, and continuing till 1851—a longer term of service than that of any of the eight or ten pastors by whom he has been succeeded. From Newport he went to the church in his native town of Fitzwilliam, where he continued until death.

While my father was a Congregationalist my mother, before marriage, had been converted to Methodism in a revival in the interest of that denomination, conducted at Northville, where meetings were held as early as 1830, in a school house, and later in a chapel, and where a society had been organized. This cause did not flourish greatly, however, till about 1850, when there was a break in the ranks of the Congregational church, and a large number went over to the Methodists, who, thus reinforced, set to work with a will and started a movement for the erection of a church building in the village, which was completed in 1851, and formally dedicated on Christmas Day, December 25, of that year.

I distinctly remember attending the dedicatory service, riding up with my father from East Unity where we then lived. It was a cold day, but the church was completely filled. The dedicatory sermon was given by Prof. King, principal of the Methodist Seminary at Newbury, Vt., who was regarded as a very able preacher, and certainly made an eloquent address on this occasion. The pastor of the church at this time was Rev. Warren F. Evans, who also held services in the school house at East Unity, near our home, about once a month, on Sunday evening at "early candle lighting," as the call announced. He made his headquarters, on these occasions at our house. Before his ministrations, one Rev. Daniel Lee, and another clergyman named Heath had served.

The Congregationalists and the Methodists by no means covered the religious field in Newport in those days. There was a Baptist church early in the history of the town, established first at Northville, but later removing to the village, where a house of worship was built at the upper end of the common about the time when the present Congregational church was erected, and where services have been conducted with general regularity to the present time. A Universalist society, which had been organized some years before, erected a church building on the West side of Main street, in 1837, in which services were held most of the time for over 30 years, after which it passed into the hands of the Unitarians, who held it a few years, when it was sold and transformed for commercial uses: since then the Catholics and Episcopalians have come to the front, the former in goodly numbers, with established places of worship.

I well remember my first visit to a store and the first purchase that I ever made. It was at the old Richards store, kept by Captain Seth Richards; afterwards Seth Richards & Son, and later Seth Richards & Sons. My father, whom I had accompanied, had given me one of the big, red copper cents, current in the olden days, but rarely seen at the present time, to spend as I saw fit, and it was with some trepidation, but no little pride, that I passed it out to a young man in attendance, then a clerk in his father's store, who subsequently became well known throughout the State as the Hon. Dexter Richards, in exchange for a stick of red and white striped candy. The consumption of that stick of candy, which lasted several days, gave more satisfaction than any later experience of the kind.

This Richards store was located in a long, two story, wooden block, built by Col. William Cheney about 1810, who had come into town from Alstead, several years before, and which occupied the site of the present Richards block. Col. Cheney, who was characterized as a man of much enterprise and public spirit, had a store in the northerly end of this block, in which he was succeeded by his son, William H. Cheney, and he by Captain Richards.

The Richards family was the most notable in Newport during the larger part of the last century, three generations of them having been prominent in the business life of the town; but it was the career of Hon. Dexter Richards, merchant, manufacturer, politician and man of affairs, that brought most distinction to the name. Retiring from trade and engaging in manufacturing, he gained a handsome fortune and did not hesitate to spend some portion of the same for the benefit of the community in the donation of a fine school building and an elegant public library. He had served in both branches of the State Legislature and in the Executive Council and might have been Governor had he been ready to contribute the amount then exacted to the party campaign fund; but, as he subsequently told the writer, he thought he could put the money to better use by building a library for the town. It may be noted in passing that the man who took the nomination and the Governorship, when Mr. Richards might have had the same, was the late Col. Charles H. Sawyer of Dover, whose veto of the famous "Hazen Bill" created such a sensation in railroad circles.

Two other general stores in Newport, which I distinctly remember as there in my early days, were those of Bela Nettleton and Mudgett & Higbee. These were on the east side of the street; the first nearly opposite the Richards store and the latter farther to the south. Bela Nettleton, Nathan Mudgett and John H. Higbee were all prominent citizens and active in the public life of the town. I knew little of either of their families, but I know that a son of the former, Lieut. Col. Edward F. Nettleton, whose death occurred recently was a gallant Union soldier in the Civil war, going out first as a Lieutenant in the company raised by Captain Ira McL. Barton; and I met, somewhere, a few years since, a lady from Newport, R. I., wife of Hon. John B. Sanborn, a prominent Rhode Island politician, who told me she was born in Newport, N. H., and that her father's name was John H. Higbee.

On a winter day, in my early life, accompanying my father to the village as I often did, we went into the county court room, where the court was then in session, to get warm and rest for a time, while the "grist," which had been taken to mill, was being ground. I had little idea of what was going on in court, but I remember distinctly, the appearance of the judge on the bench, who was none other than the Hon. Henry F. French of Exeter, then an Associate Justice of the Court of Common Pleas, as our trial courts were then called. His stern, dignified countenance, surmounted by a thick head of white hair, cut and combed a la pompadour, presented a very formidable appearance to me, which I have never forgotten. This Judge French, who subsequently held an important position in one of the departments at Washington, was an uncle of Henry F. Hollis of Concord, formerly United States Senator, and now practicing law in Paris, his sister having married Major Abijah Hollis, the Senator's father, who is still living in Concord, well and vigorous at the age of 87.

I do not recall having entered that court room again until the August term of court in 1866, when, after having attended the Michigan University Law School, at Ann Arbor, I was studying in the office of Hon. Edmund Burke, and, naturally, with other students frequented the court sessions. It was during this term, by the way, that I was formally admitted to the bar, the motion for my admission, having been made by Edmund L. Cushing of Charlestown, subsequently chief justice of the Supreme Court, and seconded by Ira Colby of Claremont.

I may as well mention the fact here as anywhere that when I was studying law in Newport, there were two other students in town, Marquis D. McCollester (who subsequently dropped the Mc from his name) and Alfred F. Howard—the former in the office of Albert S. Wait, and the latter in that of Shepard L. Bowers. What became of Collester I am unaware, but I do not think he is now living. Howard located in Portsmouth in the practice of law, which he followed successfully for a time; but subsequently went into insurance and was for many years the Secretary of the Granite State Fire Insurance Co., but died some years since. He was for a long time active in Republican politics, but refused to be a candidate for Governor or any other important office.

The active lawyers in Newport at this time were Messrs. Burke, Wait, Bowers and Levi W. Barton, though the late Judge W. H. H. Allen had an office there, but soon removed to Claremont. All these men were more or less active in politics—Burke and Wait as Democrats and Barton and Bowers as Republicans. Mr. Barton was most active at this time, and cherished a laudable ambition to represent his district in Congress, which he might have done but for the fact that two other prominent Republicans of Sullivan County cherished the same ambition at the same time—Ira Colby of Claremont and Chester Pike of Cornish—so that neither got the prize and Sullivan County was left out of the running.

At this time the venerable Amasa Edes, who was in practice at the period of my earliest recollection, had long been retired, and his son, Samuel H. Edes, grandfather of the recent editor of the Argus, had practically retired from the law and gone into manufacturing.

When I was five years of age my parents removed to East Unity, where my father had purchased what was formerly known as the Ovid Chase place, and which for many years past has been owned and occupied by Wallace Hall, a G. A. R. veteran. There were then, as now, two roads by which this place was reached from Newport, the one more commonly used being by way of Unity Springs, and the other by the Goshen road as far as the Allen place, so called, thence branching to the right. The distance from Newport village either way, was about five miles.

I well remember the day of our removal. It was one of the first days in April, 1846, and early as it was in the season, the ground was quite dry, and dust was flying in the fields along the way where farmers were at work on the land. Our nearest neighbor to the east was one Moses Wright, who had a large family of boys and one girl, while a young man named Clough, one of a numerous family of that name in the district, who had recently been married, lived in the first house on the west, at the top of the hill, near which the schoolhouse was located.

My first recollections of life in Unity center about the school, which, for the first summer of my attendance, was taught by Miss Experience R. Crossman, daughter of John Crossman, whose home was in the district and not far from the school house. The school district was a large one, embracing the entire eastern portion of the town, with some forty families, about fifty children attending school in the summer and not less than eighty in the winter, including in the latter season many full-grown young men and women. Among familiar names in the district were Gilman (of which name there were several families) Clough, Bartlett, Sanborn, Way, Gee, Wright, Thurber, Huntoon, Miles, Graves and Booth. Few of the old homesteads remain today in possession of the old families or their descendants, the Wright place being the only one that I recall. This Wright farm, then occupied by Moses Wright, had been settled upon by his father of the same name, who was a Revolutionary soldier and pensioner, soon after the close of the war, and the old house, still occupied, was built by him in 1800. His son, Moses, Jr., who was the proprietor at the time of our removal, had a family of six sons and one daughter—Warren, Weston, John, Charles, Darwin, Frank and Isabel. The oldest son, Warren, succeeded his father in the ownership, and his son, Homer, is now in possession, but he has a married son, living with him on the place, who is also married and has children, so that six successive generations have lived on the farm—a circumstance with few parallels in the county or state.

There were two families of Huntoons in the district—those of Harvey and William Huntoon, not nearly related so far as I am aware. Harvey Huntoon (generally known as the Honorable Harvey) was a leading citizen of the town and prominent in Democratic politics, having served as sheriff of the County and in other responsible positions. He had several sons and a daughter, among the names that I recall being Ruel, Ransom, Ora, Ira, Ariel and Lamira. Ransom, who served in the Union army in the Civil War, was a resident of Newport for many years previous to his death; while Ora was a long time resident of Contoocook, in Hopkinton, where he was in trade with the late Hon. Grovenor Curtis, whose daughter he had married.

William Huntoon, who lived in the extreme south-east corner of the town, had several daughters and a son, the former all grown before we moved into the district. One of these daughters was the wife of William H. McCrillis of Goshen, and mother of John McCrillis, Newport's present day prominent citizen and man of affairs; another, Amanda, was an experienced teacher and taught the school in the home district, in the second summer of our residence there. The son, Martin H., attended the school in winter, while we resided in the district. I remember him for his quiet studious habits, and his extreme good nature in spite of the mischievous pranks which some of us younger boys used to play upon him. He learned the printer's trade, and was for some time engaged in various newspaper offices; but was for some years previous to his recent death a resident of Bradford. He was a great reader, and a classical and historical student of no mean attainments.

This William Huntoon was a Whig in politics, and the only man of that political faith in the district, until my father's removal there. I well remember the visit that old "Uncle Nat" Huntoon, father of the Honorable Harvey, made to our house soon after our arrival there, to try to turn my father from the "error of his way" in matters political.

Speaking of Hon. Harvey Huntoon, I am reminded of the fact that he had a rival in Democratic leadership in Unity, in the person of Col. Ezra J. Glidden, who resided near the middle of the town, so called, and was an extensive and successful farmer, so much so indeed that his fame extended through the state, and he was for a time President of the New Hampshire Agricultural Society, at whose fairs he was a prominent exhibitor in different lines for several years. These two men, Huntoon and Glidden, were the only men considered of any account in political affairs in Unity, for a long series of years. Between them they controlled the Democratic party in the town, and there was not enough of the opposition there, then, to be of any considerable account.

One of the larger girls attending school in the winter season, here, was Mary Sanborn, daughter of Tappan Sanborn, who was the East Unity postmaster. She had been away, for a term or two, attending the N. H. Conference Seminary, then located in Northfield, where she had taken piano lessons. It used to fall to my lot to go for the mail, at the postoffice, once a week, and I remember hearing her play, on one of these occasions, it being the first time that I had ever heard a piano. This Mary Sanborn, subsequently married one John Paul, a native of the town of Wakefield, if I remember rightly, who had studied law and been admitted to the bar, and who settled in Newport, though I am not aware that he ever practiced his profession to any great extent. I think they retained the Sanborn home, and occupied it more or less of the time for several years.

The Sanborn place bordered upon Gilman's Pond, on one shore of which was an extensive blueberry swamp, which, with other children of the neighborhood, I used to visit in the blueberry season, with pleasure as well as profit. This pond was the first considerable body of water that I ever saw, and I well remember the excitement I experienced on catching the first fish which I took from its waters, which were remarkably pure and clear, and which have since been utilized as a water-supply for the village of

ident of the United States.

I have mentioned the fact that Miss Experience R. Crossman, who subsequently became the wife of Matthew Harvey, for nearly forty years associated with H. G. Carleton in the publication of the old Argus and Spectator, was the teacher of the East Unity school during the first summer of my attendance, and that Amanda M. Huntoon taught the following summer. Both of these accomplished young ladies were residents of the district. Following them was another young woman, also a resident—Clarinda C. Currier—for whom I conceived a strong boyish admiration, on account of her pleasant manner and charming personality. It was when Miss Currier was the teacher, and it became necessary for me to have a new spelling book, on account of a change of text books in the school, that I was entrusted with a dime by my mother and authorized to go to the nearest store, which was at what is now known as Mill Village, in the town of Goshen, and buy the desired volume.

I was then seven years of age, and started off, one Saturday afternoon, with a decided feeling of exaltation at the importance of my errand and the responsibility attached. The distance to the store was a little over a mile, by a hilly road, past the Wright farm and the Harvey Huntoon place, and by the homes of Frances Jane Miles and Emma Gilman, two of the prettiest girls in school, which I passed with some interest, and soon found myself over the river (Sugar River south branch) and at the store, kept by one Virgil Chase, from whom I secured a Town's speller in exchange for my small silver coin which I had carried with much care. I must confess that, upon examination, I was not greatly elated with my prize. It seemed to me that the Town's speller was decidedly inferior to the old Webster's spelling book which it had been destined to displace; and that not entirely on account of the interesting pictures that adorned the latter, among which was that of the boy stealing apples, whom the old man was trying to bring down from the tree. I am still of the opinion that Webster's was the better book.

This Virgil Chase, the store-keeper, as I learned in later years, was a "big man" in his community and well known throughout the county. He had held most of the town offices, been sheriff of the county, and was a prominent Democratic party leader. It was for him that Virgil C. Gilman, who was born in the neighborhood and became a prominent citizen of Nashua and leading Republican politician in the State was named. I never saw him again, to be aware of the fact, until early in 1859, when I was about eighteen years of age, and deeply impressed with the importance of doing what I could to stay the onward march of the Republican party, in its determination to rule the country. I prepared and committed an elaborate speech, and started out to deliver the same wherever opportunity offered. One of the chosen places was Mill Village, Goshen, where I arrived on an early March evening, and was entertained in the home of this same Virgil Chase, then somewhat advanced in years, but mentally and bodily vigorous, and as staunch in his Democracy as ever. The meeting, which was held in the school house, had been well advertised and the room was filled. Mr. Chase presided, introduced me with some appropriate remarks, and I delivered my speech, to the best of my ability and without interruption. As I concluded, amid some applause, a young man arose and asked the privilege of answering me, from the Republican standpoint. This was one Ira McL. Barton, a son of Levi W. Barton of Newport, who with a fellow law-student, one Joseph Wood, of Alstead, a brother of the late Col. James A. Wood, had heard of the meeting, and come down from Newport to "do me up."

Mr. Chase demurred to the proposition, saying it was a Democratic meeting and no place for opposition propaganda, or words to that effect; and cries of "throw them out" were started; but, duly impressed with righteousness of the cause, I urged him to let the young men proceed, which he ultimately did, and after they had unloaded themselves, both Mr. Chase and myself proceeded, as we were fully satisfied, however it may have been with the audience, to demolish their arguments and establish the absolute justice and righteousness of the Democratic cause.

I have referred to some of the summer teachers in the East Unity school which I attended during the residence of our family in that locality, from the time when I was five to eleven years of age. Somehow I have a clearer recollection of the summer, or female, teachers, than of the men who had charge of the school in the winter season, when it required a man of muscle as well as brains to maintain order, and hold in proper subjection the seventy-five or eighty scholars, among whom were a dozen fully grown boys not all inclined to be docile and orderly.

One of these male teachers, whom I now recall, was one Otis Heath, a son of the Methodist clergyman who was then preaching in Newport, with an occasional service in the East Unity school house on Sunday evenings. Otis was a lively young man and quite a favorite with the boys and girls of whom there were many in the school; but he had the boys in proper subjection only by occasional application of the ferrule. He was somewhat foppish in dress and occasionally wore a tall silk hat. One day, at the noon hour, one of the large boys, the oldest one in school in fact, one Alexis J. Graves, took possession of this hat, went into the adjoining field, and, climbing a tall tree, broke off the top of an upright limb and hung the hat thereon. The master had his eye on him all the while, however, and, when the time for the afternoon recess came, stopped him as the boys went out, and calmly but firmly told him to get and return that hat, with which command he deemed it best to comply. This Alexis J. Graves, by the way, and his interesting family, were living in Newport, nearly twenty years later, when I was studying law in the village.

Another one of the "big boys" in school at this time, whom I distinctly remember, was Silas M. Gee, whose people lived in the last house in Unity, on the Newport road, passing Unity Springs. My recollection is that he was an only son. At all events he inherited and passed his life upon the home place, and was a thrifty farmer. I knew little of him, however, until, some twenty years ago, when I was reporting the proceedings of the State Legislature for the Portsmouth Times, he turned up in the House as a Representative from Unity, which town, although strictly Democratic in the early days, had become close, politically, and was sometimes carried by the Republicans, to which party Gee belonged. Of course we soon found each other out, and together recalled the days when he from the back seat, and I from one of the front ones, in the old school room, imbibed such measure of wisdom as our differing capacities enabled us to gather in.

One of the large families in this East Unity school district, was the Booth family, with several sons and two or three daughters, the name of only one of the latter being recalled by me. This was Harriet, a black-eyed, red-cheeked girl, of whose life in after days I knew nothing. Of the boys I remember the names of Adolphus, Charles, Marvin, Rollin or Roland and Burke. These all scattered ultimately, and I never knew the fate or whereabouts of all of them. I am of the impression that Adolphus settled in Walpole, while Charles was long a resident of the town of Lempster. Burke, the youngest of the family, was a long time resident and prominent citizen of Goshen.

This Booth family lived on the south road, near the Lempster line, midway between the Benjamin Graves family, to which Alexis J., before mentioned, belonged, and that of his brother, John Graves, who was an active Methodist. Of the John Graves family I remember but a daughter and son, Rhoda and Bela, both considerably older than myself, but attendants of the school in the winter season. Rhoda boarded at our house during the school term, so as to be near the school house. Bela occupied the home place during his life time and became a prosperous farmer. He was particularly active in the Grange, and, if I mistake not, was at one time a member of the

State Board of Agriculture. He passed away some years since.

It was after a meeting called in the school house in East Unity, when I was eight or ten years of age, that I heard the first political address, or "stump speech," to which I ever had the privilege of listening. I do not recall who presided at this gathering, though I surmise that it was the Democratic political "boss" of the district, Hon. Harvey Huntoon, nor do I remember much that the speaker said, although I recall that he spoke with a decided brogue. This speaker was William C. Sturoc, who was then studying law at Newport, in Edmund Burke's office. He had recently come into the country from Scotland, with the intention of making his home here, and was seeking to familiarize himself with our institutions and laws. He naturally imbibed the political views of his instructor and became an ardent Democrat. It was in the interests of this party that he was then speaking. Mr. Sturoc settled in Sunapee, where he opened a law office, but was never extensively engaged in practice. He subsequently married an elderly lady there, who had quite a farm, the cultivation of which he enjoyed, and spent his leisure hours in reading and writing verse, in which latter line he was quite proficient, some of his poems ranking with the finest in the language. He was for several years, along in the sixties, a Representative in the Legislature from the town of Sunapee, and was among the active Democratic leaders in that body at a time when partisan feeling was at its height. He was for many years prominent in Democratic State Conventions, and his services on the stump were in great demand in political campaigns. He had made great progress in speaking ability since that first effort in the East Unity school house.

I knew Mr. Sturoc well in later years, meeting him frequently in his Sunapee home and elsewhere, and on the last occasion was charged with the duty of writing his obituary when he should pass away, which he did a dozen years ago or more.

As I have before mentioned our nearest neighbors to the east in Unity were the Wright family. The three older sons were all stalwart boys, some six feet in height, but all attended the winter school. Charles was about my age and my chosen companion and playmate.

Mrs. Wright's maiden name was Esther Thrasher. She was a daughter of John Thrasher, of Cornish, who made frequent visits at the Wright home. He was a man of much native talent and had been well educated, but his habits were such that he had not made the success in life that he might otherwise have attained. One of his sons was that Samuel P. Thrasher of Plainfield, who was elected to the state senate and died before the meeting of the Legislature, leaving a vacancy which was filled through the choice by that body of Alvah Smith of Lempster. This was during one of the Weston administrations, when the Democrats and Labor Reformers had a majority in the House and with Smith's vote would have controlled the Senate. Smith had but four votes at the polls, as the Labor Reform candidate, but stood next to the defeated Republican candidate, Albina Hall of Grantham, and was chosen by the Democrats in the Legislature with the understanding that he would act with them, which, after being seated, he refused to do, much to their disappointment and disgust. He had formerly been an active Republican, and his old time associates of that party got hold of him, fed him up with promises and controlled his action. Soon after one of his sons was made U. S. Pension agent for New Hampshire.

When my only sister, Ella, who was three and a half years my junior, was about five years old, she climbed up to a beam in the shed one day, from which she fell on to a loose pile of wood, striking her head on a sharp stick, and cutting a bad jash in the scalp and slightly fracturing the skull. An artery was severed by the cut, and the bleeding was profuse. My mother was unable to stanch the wound and father hastened to Newport for a doctor. He obtained the services of Dr. Thomas Sanborn, one of the three physicians then practicing there, who soon secured the artery and properly dressed the wound.

This Dr. Sanborn, who practiced in Newport from 1842, till his death in 1875, became noted as a skillful surgeon, in which capacity he served in the 16th N. H. Regiment in the Civil War. Contemporaneous with him in practice in Newport, for many years, were Drs. John L. Swett and Mason Hatch. Dr. Swett, who was a native of Claremont, and a graduate of the Jefferson Medical College of Philadelphia, settled in the town in 1826, and remained through life, continuing in active practice for more than half a century. He gained high rank in his profession, and was at one time President of the N. H. Medical Society. Many young men studied for the profession with him, one of whom was my eldest brother, Carlos G., five years younger than myself, who was born shortly after our removal to East Unity. He subsequently graduated from the Albany Medical College, practiced in Troy, N. H., Middleton, East Douglas, and Marlboro, Mass., and died in the latter town in 1884, at the age of 38 years.

Newport's first settled physician was Dr. James Corbin, who located in town about 1790, and continued in practice till his death in 1826, though in the later years of his life he devoted much attention to agriculture, in which he was greatly interested, having purchased a large farm some two miles above the village toward

Northville. He was a native of Dudley, Mass., and was the father of Austin Corbin, Sr., as we may have heretofore mentioned.

Succeeding, and for a time contemporaneous with Dr. Corbin, in practice, was Dr. John B. McGregor, a native of the town, and member of a prominent family, who had been a student in his office. He was in practice in Newport from 1810 till 1828, when he removed to Rochester, N. Y. Dr. McGregor was a great lover of music and a devoted patron of the art. It is a matter of history that the first piano brought into the town of Newport was purchased by Dr. McGregor for his daughter, Marion, who ultimately became one of the most accomplished musicians in the country, serving for 25 years as organist for Broadway Tabernacle, New York City.

Here it may be mentioned that much musical talent has been developed in Newport along both vocal and instrumental lines in years past. Especially has the music at the South Congregational Church been noted for its excellence with organists and choir singers of superior ability, as a rule. It is a source of special pride to the people of the town, that Nelson P. Coffin, who became one of the most eminent and successful oratorio and festival conductors in the country, though dying deeply lamented at a comparatively early age, was born, reared, educated and commenced his brilliant career in Newport.

One of the delightful occasions of the country small boy in the olden days, was the annual fall muster of the militia. Under the old state militia system, in vogue 75 years ago and more, every able bodied man in the state, between the ages of 18 and 45 with certain specific exceptions, was enrolled in the service, and twice during the year was called upon to report for duty in drill and discipline. The first occasion was the spring training, when, sometime in the month of May, the men met in companies, and were drilled by their officers; while the second, and more important event of the year, was the regimental muster, when all the companies in the district came together at the stated muster ground, and were put through the prescribed evolutions by the regimental officers, and were usually inspected by the brigade or division commander.

The fall muster day was a holiday occasion for all the surrounding country. No man with a heart in him, who had any young boys, failed to provide some means for their attendance, and the boy who could not attend was a most unhappy mortal. As it happened, my father, who was not married till somewhat late in life, was past the age for military service, and, not having to participate in the exercises, could attend as a spectator, and take me along, as a matter of course, a privilege which I highly enjoyed.

The "Common" in Newport village was the

usual muster ground for the larger part of Sullivan County. In those days it was much larger than at present, extending back to the rise of ground at the east, and including all the land covered by the buildings now there, except the space occupied by one large four-story tenement block, which I remember as painted a dingy yellow, and generally known as the old "Tontine," but how the name originated I am unable to say. This building stood about where the Methodist church and the two dwellings to the north of the same now stand, if I remember rightly. The splendid rows of maples, surrounding the present common, making it one of the most attractive village commons in New England, had not then been set out, so that there was ample opportunity for military evolutions on a large scale.

The last of these fall musters that I remember attending, was when I was some ten years of age, and was an unusual occasion, since there were three regiments participating, and a correspondingly large attendance of spectators. It was a beautiful autumn day. All sorts of venders surrounded the grounds, but those attracting most attention from the younger element were the sellers of gingerbread and sweet cider, the standard price for the latter being one cent a glass. Although a Concord municipal court justice has recently ruled that a man may lawfully manufacture all the sweet cider he pleases, no one would be likely to exercise his right in this regard to a very great extent if he had to dispose of his product at the price prevalent in those days.

The evolutions of the several regiments on this occasion were more or less intricate and interesting to the spectators, old and young, and the exercises of the day closed with a "sham fight", which I recollect as characterized by much noise and great clouds of smoke of decidedly sulphurous nature, artillery as well as infantry participating.

I have often thought, and still believe that if we are to continue preparing for war in time of peace, as the militarists of the present day insist should be the case, the old time militia system, under which all able-bodied men were compelled to bear arms and to train in their use, to some extent, is preferable to the present system, under which a small body known as the National Guard, is more highly trained.

Even more interesting than the fall muster, to old and young, male and female alike, were the old time County fairs, or "cattle shows," as they were generally called, because the exhibition of neat cattle was the main feature of the show, though horses, sheep and swine were exhibited in goodly numbers. The Sullivan County fair was always held in Claremont, where there were more ample grounds, and which was really more accessible than Newport for that portion of the county making the greatest exhibit in the different lines, both of animal and agricultural products, namely the towns in the Connecticut valley, Charlestown, Claremont, Cornish and Plainfield. Claremont always ranked as one of the four or five best agricultural towns in the state, especially in corn production, Walpole in Cheshire County, and Haverhill in Grafton, being competitors; while Plainfield stood at the head in sheep and wool production.

I remember attending one of these County fairs at Claremont when there were 320 yoke of oxen on the ground; more than can be found in half the counties of the state at the present time, if not in the entire state. This was in the days of "town teams," when there was lively competition among the towns, to see which could bring out the largest team in proportion to population. I distinctly remember that it was said the town of Croydon, even then as now, one of the smallest in the county in point of population, had a team of 80 yoke of oxen on the ground, or one quarter of the entire exhibit in that line.

This Croydon team had been gotten together through the enterprise and energy of Moses Humphrey, then a leading citizen of the town, though he had come up from Hingham, Mass., where he was born and reared to a sea-faring life as a fisherman, only some two or three years previously. "Uncle Moses", as he was familiarly known throughout the State in later years, was a man of great ambition and untiring energy, and had been the master of a fishing vessel while yet in his minority. He married a Croydon girl and migrated to that town in early life, engaging in the manufacture of mackerel kits at the "Flat"; but his public spirit and zeal for progress directed his attention in other directions also and made him a leader in town affairs generally. This, by the way, was before the late Ruel Durkee had come to the fore as Croydon's master mind and directing genius.

While speaking of Moses Humphrey, we may as well note the fact that his residence in Croydon was comparatively brief, though his love for the old town always remained strong, and he seldom failed to attend the "Old People's Meetings," held there for many years before "Old Home Day" was instituted by Gov. Frank Rollins, in which they have since been merged, with a gathering once in three years. After a few years he left Croydon for Concord, and established his business at the West Village; but branched out in other directions, acquiring some land and developing much interest in agriculture, particularly in corn culture. He also began to interest himself in public affairs, was elected to the city council and was soon made Mayor of the City, holding that office during the first two years of the Civil war and again, in 1865, when the soldiers returned from the conflict, and was as actively interested in welcoming them home as he had been in furthering their departure. He it was who originated and developed the Concord Street Railway, and fathered the Act establishing the State Board of Agriculture, of which he became the first President, holding the office till about 90 years of age, and giving to the discharge of its duties more of zeal and energy than many a younger man could have shown.

Reference has been made to the fact that "Uncle Moses" Humphrey took a team of 80 yoke of oxen from the town of Croydon to a Sullivan County Fair at Claremont, which I attended in my early boyhood. Located in a mountain region, with a rugged and rocky surface, Croydon was inhabited in the olden days by a thrifty and industrious class of people, who succeeded in winning a good livelihood despite adverse circumstances, and among them were a number of really prosperous farmers, notable among them being John Putnam, father of the Ellen Putnam whom I mentioned as one of my first teachers, and of George F. Putnam, a prominent lawyer and Democratic politician.

This George F. Putnam, by the way, was not the only prominent lawyer or man of distinction native of Croydon or born of Croydon stock. The late Hon. Wilbur H. Powers of Boston, orator of the day at the town's 150th anniversary in

1916; Hon. Wliliam P. Wheeler, of Keene, president of the day at its 100th anniversary celebration in 1866 and Hon. Levi W. Barton, long in practice in Newport, and father of Judge Jesse M. Barton, present leading attorney of the town and county, were all born in Croydon; while those two eminent Boston lawyers, Samuel L. Powers, and Sherman L. Whipple, both came of Croydon stock, their fathers having been born in the town.

My first recollections of Croydon are of visits to my grandmother Metcalf, living with my uncle Moses Metcalf on the old homestead cleared up by my grandfather, Captain Obed Metcalf, who died before my birth, leaving a widow, my grandmother; whom I frequently visited, with my parents, such visits always being a source of pleasure, especially in the season when fruit was ripening, the farm producing a variety of fine fruit. This farm, along with more than a third of all the farms in town, is now abandoned and included within the limits of Corbin Park or Blue Mountain Park as it is more often called, which also included a large section of Cornish and Grantham.

Since the death of my grandfather, who lived to the good old age of 88 years, and the removal of my uncle's family to the West, I have visited Croydon only on public occasions. I attended the town's 100th anniversary celebration in 1866, at which Hon. William P. Wheeler presided, as previously mentioned, and at which the oration was delivered by Rev. Baron Stowe, eminent Baptist divine of Boston, born near the base of the mountain, and with whom, when a boy I have heard my father tell of fishing in the mountain brooks. He was a speaker of rare eloquence, and held the large crowd in attendance spell bound during his address.

For the last thirty years or more I have attended the Old Home Day gatherings in the town, originally known as Old People's Day meeting, the same having been instituted long before Gov. Rollins established Old Home Day, as was the case also in the town of Cornish. Once in three years is as often as these gatherings are now held in Croydon, the burden of annual gatherings being too much for the limited population of the town, especially as a free dinner is served to the crowd in attendance.

On one occasion, not of a public nature, I made a visit to Croydon. This was on a beautiful autumn day some twenty-five years ago, when I was accompanied by the late Hon. Stillman Humphrey, a former mayor of Concord, native of the town and nephew of the "Uncle Moses", heretofore mentioned. We made the trip from Concord for the purpose of ascending the mountain, going up to Newport by train and taking a team from a livery, there, for the base of the mountain, driving through the park and well up into the notch, by the old road over the mountain to Cornish. A climb of about three-quarters of a mile from the road brought us to the summit from which the view, though not as extended as that from Kearsarge or Monadnock, was most satisfactory, well repaying the labor involved in the journey and ascent.

Croydon's most noted resident, Ruel Durkee, the Jethro Bass of Winston Churchill's famous novel, "Coniston", whose principal scene was laid in this town, was never met by me in Croydon, but I often saw him in Concord, during the legislative sessions, as he wandered through the lobbies at the "Pelican", arrayed in his tall hat and "swallow-tailed" coat, muttering inaudibly to himself.

The Sullivan County town with which I am least familiar, and which I never visited in my boyhood, although born within a quarter of a mile of its southwest corner, is the town of Cornish, noted in these later days as the resort of an aristocratic summer colony; long the home of St. Gaudens, the sculptor, and of Winston Churchill, the novelist, who instituted the Progressive movement in Republican politics, into which Robert P. Bass and others entered with such effect that they brought about a partial Democratic victory in 1913. It was in this town, and at Churchill's residence, "Harlakenden", that President Woodrow Wilson established the "summer capital" during the first year of his incumbency, this being the first and only time that New Hampshire has been honored in this way.

It was Cornish that gave birth to Philander Chase, noted Episcopal Bishop who became a power in his church in the Middle West, and the distinguished statesman and jurist, Salmon P. Chase, Governor of Ohio, U. S. Senator, Secretary of the Treasury during the Civil War, and finally Chief Justice of the Supreme Court of the United States.

Here also was born Samuel L. Powers, Boston lawyer, to whom reference has heretofore been made, general counsel of the New England Telephone and Telegraph Company and former Reprensentative in Congress, son of Larnard Powers who emigrated from Croydon in early life. Another son was Erastus B. Powers, who was a teacher for some years, but ultimately engaged in the practice of law in Boston.

A prominent family in Cornish was the Jackson family, whose most distinguished member at the time of my boyhood was Eleazer Jackson, generally known as Judge Jackson, he having been a Judge of the Common Pleas Court. He was an active Democrat and prominent in public affairs. A sister of his was the wife of Austin Corbin, Sr., of Newport, and mother of the famous brothers, Austin, Daniel and James Corbin.

About fifty-five years ago, when employed on the "People" newspaper in Concord, I made a trip to Cornish in the interests of the paper, seeking to extend the circulation, and was entertained at the Jackson home, then occupied by Charles E. Jackson, a son of Judge George and an active Democrat, whom I had frequently met at meetings of the Democratic State Committee, of which he was a member. He accompanied me about among the people of the town, and the result was a satisfactory addition to the subscription list of the paper.

Another prominent citizen of Cornish, whom I knew well years ago, was Col. Chester Pike who was prominent in agricultural circles and in Republican politics. He was a leading member of the Sullivan County Agricultural Society, holding its fairs at Claremont, was Collector of Internal Revenue for the Third District, had been President of the State Senate, and aspired to a seat in Congress, at the same time that two other Sullivan County men, Levi W. Barton of Newport and Ira Colby, Jr., of Claremont cherished similar aspirations, with the result that neither ever succeeded.

Upon one other occasion I visited Cornish. It was about 25 years ago, when a Farmers' Institute was held at the Center under the auspices of the State Board of Agriculture, N. J.

Bachelder, the Secretary, being the directing spirit. I had been in the habit of accompanying the speakers at these institutes to report the meetings for the press, and it so happened that I was occasionally called upon to speak, as was the case at the opening of the afternoon session at this Cornish meeting. In commenting upon the work of the Board, and particularly upon the earnest labor of the Secretary, I took occasion to suggest that if the Republican party wanted to do a good thing for itself and for the State, it would nominate Secretary Bachelder for Governor, which, by the way, it did in the following year.

Reference to the recent mention in the Argus-Champion of the plan for the erection of some memorial to Mrs. Sarah J. Hale, formerly Sarah Josepha Buell, reputed author of "Mary's Little Lamb", near the site of the old school house, to which the lamb is supposed to have followed her on a summer day, leads me to speak of Mrs. Hale, though I knew nothing of her personally, and of some other Newport people of note in the world at large.

Bereaved by the death of her husband, David Hale, a young lawyer, in comparatively early life, Mrs. Hale found herself thrown upon her own resources for support, and resorted in the first instance to the millinery business, opening a shop wherein she catered to the then fashionable circle of the town. Not finding this business sufficiently remunerative, and being gifted with literary ability, she secured an engagement for magazine work with a Boston publisher, and was there for a time employed; but soon attracted the attention of Louis A. Godey of Philadelphia, who made her editor of his famous "Lady's Book," the first distinctive woman's magazine in the country, which position she held for nearly 40 years, winning a high reputation in the American literary world, and taking a strong interest in public affairs. To Mrs. Hale belongs the credit for the establishment of National Thanksgiving Day, President Grant having issued the proclamation for the first observance of the kind in response to her repeated appeals.

Mrs. Hale was not the only woman of note and achievement whom Newport furnished to the world. Reference has already been made to Malvina Chapin Rowell, missionery to Hawaii or the Sandwich Islands, and Marion McGregor, noted musician, long time organist at the Broadway Temple, New York, but a still more prominent figure in the country's life was Helen Peabody, born in Newport early in the last century, educated in Mary Lyon's school at Mount Holyoke, now Mount Holyoke College, who was called to the presidency of the first distinctive woman's college in the country, that of Western College at Oxford, Ohio, which position she held for forty years, with eminent success, having declined a call to the presidency of Wellesley, when that institution was opened, which position was filled by another New Hampshire woman, Ada Howard, native of Temple.

Referring to Newport's contribution to the country's public and business life, we have heretofore mentioned the brilliant careers of the three famous Corbin brothers, Austin, Daniel and James; also those of Kendrick Metcalf, long time Professor of Latin in Hobart College, and Carlos Gould, who was a pioneer Methodist preacher in Western New York; but particular reference should be made to the public service of Hon. Edmund Burke, who came to town in early life as editor of the Argus, and made Newport his home throughout the balance of his days. He served the State and Nation with distinction as a member of Congress for six years from 1839 to 1845, and was Commissioner of Patents under President Polk from 1845 to 1849, after which he was for a time editor of the Washington Union, the national Democratic paper, for which he had previously contributed the series of essays upon the tariff, over the signature of "Bundlecund," upon which the Walker tariff was based. While Commissioner of Patents he organized the Bureau of Agriculture, and issued its first report. When the N. H. State Board of Agriculture was organized in 1871, he was made the Sullivan County member of the same.

Another citizen of Newport to attain distinction was Ralph Metcalf, who became Governor of New Hampshire in 1855, as the candidate of the New American, otherwise known as the Know Nothing Party, made up of the remnants of the old Whig party, the Abolitionists and Free Soil Democrats, which the next year changed its name to the Republican party, and re-elected Gov. Metcalf, who afterwards removed to Claremont.

Among Newport born men, publicly conspicuous was Rear Admiral George E. Belknap, one of the most eminent officers of the American Navy, who was appointed to Annapolis through the instrumentality of Hon. Edmund Burke, and had a brilliant career in the service during and after the Civil War.

Another Newport native to attain public prominence was Edwin O. Stannard, who went West in early life, and finally located in St. Louis, Mo., where he successfully engaged in flour manufacture. He served in Congress and was at one time Lieutenant Governor of Missouri. He was a man of fine personal appearance, and agreeable manners, as I well recall, having met him when as President of the Chamber of Commerce, he greeted the N. H. Delegation to the Democratic National convention in St. Louis, in 1876.

As I have previously stated, my father moved from Newport to East Unity in the spring of 1846, when I was five years of age, his object being to get on to a larger farm, where he could secure a better return for his labor, and on the Ovid Chase place so-called, upon which he moved, it being the farm now and for many years heretofore occupied by Wallace Hall, he was able to do this. It was a good dairy farm, upon which he kept half a dozen cows. My mother was a good butter maker, and got the reputation of being as good in that line as any woman in the county. They sold considerable butter and some cheese, and usually sold a few potatoes and some other things, so that they cleared up a small sum every year. I have a distinct recollection of my father having loaned Dexter Richards at one time $200 to use in his business—a perfectly safe investment. It seems almost amusing now, when I reflect that thirty years later, after my father had died, a comparatively poor man, Dexter Richards was reckoned a millionaire and considered the richest man in the county.

In the winter of 1851-2, the district school was taught by one Josiah H. Straw, who lived in a small brick house, opposite the Huntoon house. He was a middle aged man, and had taught school many terms in other places. The school was not as large as it had been, some of the older scholars having dropped out; but there were 70 of them at least, and strict lines of discipline had to be drawn, but Mr. Straw, although not a large man physically, was entirely equal to the situation. I recall that the teacher offered a prize of a silver half dollar to the scholar in my spelling class, who should get to the head the most times during the term. There turned out to be sharp rivalry between Ora M. Huntoon, who was two years my senior, and myself. We kept pretty nearly together, and soon out distanced all the rest, so that there was no hope for any other; and the rest of the class resolved themselves into two parties, one favoring Huntoon and the other me. The Huntoon "rooters" would let him get above them at every opportunity, and those who favored me would act accordingly. At the end we were pretty near even, though I was confident in my own mind that I was one or two ahead. The master, however, said that as we both had made a good fight and were about even, he would divide the prize; so we got a quarter apiece. What I did with mine I do not remember; but I do not forget that Huntoon subsequently became a prominent business man in Contoocook, and that a son of his was subsequently equally prominent.

Early in April, 1852, my people made their next removal, having sold the East Unity farm to one Francis J. Newton for $1050.00, and bought a place in Lempster for $800.00. This was not a change for the better from an agricultural point of view or any other. There was about fifty acres of land of a poor quality, largely light and sandy, easily cultivated and the product easily harvested, for there was not much of it, but there was a comfortable house on the place, in fairly good condition, which seems to have been its principal recommendation. The Unity place was sold, in fact, because the house was getting badly out of repair, and it was manifest that a new one must soon be built—an enterprise that my father did not care to undertake.

This place sat in from the highway running from Newport to Marlow, about two miles below East Lempster or the "Pond" as the little village was called. The nearest neighboring place, which also sat in from the highway, was that of Capt. Benajah A. Miner or "Uncle Ames", as he was commonly called, a strong bodied, strong minded individual, who could do more work than two ordinary men, and was endowed with more common sense than an average half dozen. He was the father of one son and four daughters, the son being the Rev. Alonzo A. Miner, D. D., the eminent Universalist clergyman, of Boston. It was on either the third or fourth day of April that our removal to Lempster took place, and on the night of that day there was a heavy snowfall.

An amusing incident occurred soon after our arrival at the new house. At nearly bed-time one evening the outside door was suddenly opened, and in rushed three small boys, the oldest exclaiming, "We got here", "We got here". The boys were two young sons of Moses Wright, our nearest Unity neighbor, Darwin and Frank, and another neighbor's boy, all somewhere in the vicinity of six and eight years of age. My mother got them something to eat and finally made them up a bed on the kitchen floor; but they had no more than fairly got settled down, than there was another and more vigorous rapping on the door and in came Mr. Wright and the other irate parent, who had surmised the destination of the runaways, and started in pursuit. They were promptly routed out and started on the return, being impelled over the road, I apprehend, judging from what was said, by a vigorous application of the "oil of birch."

One day in the spring, after the snow had all disappeared, except one big drift near the summit, my sister and my brother, Carl, then six years of age, set out with myself for the summit of the mountain, a pretty stiff climb especially for the small boy; but the wonderful view spread out before us in all directions, fully compensated for the effort. It was my first experience in mountain climbing, and though I have since stood on Monadnock, Kearsarge, Cardigan, Moosilauke, LaFayette, Washington and various other New Hampshire mountains, affording extended and magnificent views, I have never been so impressed with the beauty of the scene, as when I stood on the summit of Silver Mountain, now a seemingly insignificant height, on that fair day in May, 1852.

Down the south eastern slope of the mountain near the lake, was the house in which the late Dr. Carl A. Allen, the pioneer in camp life at Echo lake, was born. He was four years of age at this time; but it was not till many years later that I knew anything about him, his neighborhood and ours being separated by the mountain.

Before alluding to matters personal to myself, I may as well make some comment concerning the town of Lempster, and some of the people then residing there. Located in the center of the Southern tier of Sullivan County towns, with a territory of about 30 square miles of land, mostly rough, and of scarcely average fertility, although including some fairly productive farms, Lempster was never accounted a wealthy town, or even a prosperous town from a material point of view, but held high rank, for a long period of years for the high character and general intelligence of its people, having superior schools and having produced a large number of teachers, clergymen, and other professional men of high rank.

There was never any great amount of manufacturing in town, though at one time some business was done in the manufacture of hand rakes, in the north eastern part of the town, while, later, Alvah Smith operated a shoe factory, in connection with his tannery at "The Street," as the West

Village, the more important business place in town, was called. This village, which is located on a single long street, lately known as "Maple Street," because of the fine rows of maple trees on either side, which, by the way, have come into existance since I first knew the town, contained some twenty-five or thirty dwellings, a Congregational church edifice, an old church building which had been transformed into a town hall below, and a school room above; also a general store, a blacksmith's shop, and some other small establishments, aside from the tannery and the shoe shop, previously mentioned. There was also a very good hotel, kept by one Erastus Nichols, who had a wide reputation as a popular landlord.

The most pretentious residence in the village was a two story brick house owned and occupied by Dr. Jacob N. Butler, who was the town physician, and the only one, for nearly half a century. He was a "safe and sane" doctor of the old school; knew everybody in town, and was beloved and respected by all. He "passed to the Great Beyond" a number of years ago; but his residence still stands, though like several others in the village, it is unoccupied except for a few months in the summer season, when the family of his son, Arthur Butler, a successful civil engineer of Chicago, occupy it as a summer home. The blacksmith's shop was occupied for a time by one Lemuel Miller, a superior workman, who did most of the business in his line for the people of a wide territory, extending beyond the town limits. Here had been the home of one Dr. Truman Abell, who was more famous for the almanac that he published for a number of years, than for his skill in medicine; but he had passed "off the stage" before my day. The house which he occupied still remains. The general store was owned and conducted by one Abner Chase, who was a leading man in town affairs, and a prominent member of the Methodist church. He was a good man and had a son, and daughter, Eliza, who was highly educated and married a prominent Methodist clergyman, named Calvin Harrington, who held numerous important pastorates, and became a professor in Wesleyen University, at Middletown, Conn., where a son of theirs is now similarly located.

Two miles east of "The Street," and near the geographical center of Lempster, was, and is, a smaller village, now called East Lempster, but then generally known as "The Pond," from the fact that its location is near a small pond, sometimes called Dodge Pond, which is the source of Dodge Brook, the east branch of Cold River. There were only about a dozen dwellings in the village at this time and there has been no appreciable increase up to the present day. A Methodist church was the prominent feature of the place, which still remains, though not regularly occupied.

Across the square from the Methodist church, in the center of which square now stands a granite monument erected in memory of the men of Lempster who lost their lives in the Civil War, was a small chapel occupied by the Universalist Society for religious purposes. With some slight interior changes it remains about the same as it was 75 years ago, but services are held in it only for a few weeks during the summer vacation period.

It may as well be stated here that about 1857 the town changed its "capital," erecting a new town house at "The Pond", which, being near the center, was more conveniently reached by a majority of the citizens than "The Street." This village, by the way, is located on the Newport and Marlow road, now a state highway.

Near the Pond village, and between it and the pond itself, is located the town cemetery, or "burying ground", as it was generally called, within whose limits repose the remains of a large share of the people who have been permanent residents of the town, from the time of its first settlement, about 1767, to the present period, it being the only cemetery in town.

Speaking of farms, I have said there were a few fairly good ones in town. One of the best and largest was the Deacon Bingham place, about three-fourths of a mile north of "The

Street", on the road to Newport, via Unity Springs. This was a well kept and well cultivated farm in the days of the Deacon, who was a "pillar" in the Congregational Church and had two accomplished daughters, one of whom sang in the choir, and subsequently married one Joseph Barrett, who lived for a time on the farm, but subsequently removed to West Concord, where both died some years since.

The Bingham farm was not only the best in town, but the dwelling thereon was, in its day, by far the finest residence in Lempster. It had been built by the Deacon's father in the early days of the town. It was a large, square, square roofed, two story building, and the seat of a generous hospitality a century ago and more. It is said that Daniel Webster, who was a college-mate of James H. Bingham, was a frequent visitor here.

In mentioning some of the people resident in Lempster, when I went there, I may properly commence with the school district in which we located, which was known as District No. 7. Our nearest neighbor, whom I have previously incidentally mentioned, and really the most prominent man in the district, was Benajah A. Miner, a man of strong intellect, and wonderful physical power and energy. He was of rather austere demeanor, determined in purpose, but kind-hearted and greatly esteemed by those who knew him best. By industry and skill he had made a good living on a rather poor farm, and reared a family of one son and four daughters.

The son was the Rev. Dr. Alonzo A. Miner, one of the ablest and most distinguished clergymen of New England, who after a short pastorate in Lowell, went to Boston, and succeeded the Rev. Hosea Ballou, another New Hampshire born clergyman of note, in the pastorate of the School Street Universalist Church, whose location was subsequently removed to Columbus Avenue. The Doctor was generally regarded as the ablest preacher in Boston and when, at one time, it was deemed expedient, by the clergy of the city, to have some one defend Christianity from the assaults of the Agnostics led by Robert J. Ingersoll, he was selected by his ministerial brethren of all denominations, for the task, and most ably performed it. Dr. Miner was an early and earnest temperance advocate, and a leader of the Prohibition party in its early days. The late Patrick A. Collins, once Mayor of the city, is reputed to have remarked when some one spoke to him about the Doctor's activities—"Dr. Miner is a good man, and all right if he would only let rum alone."

The four daughters of Benajah A. Miner, were Amanda, Emma Eliza, Rachel and Fanny, all of whom were married and lived in the district during my residence there. Amanda married William B. Parker, a prominent citizen and leading Democrat, who lived on the Marlow road very near where the side road turned in for our home and that of Mr. Miner. The Parker family, of which he was a member, was one of no little importance, one brother being Benjamin Parker, father of the Hon. Hosea W. and Hiram Parker, of whom mention will be hereafter made, and another, Jonas, being a leading citizen of Goshen, residing on the Newport road, just north of Mill Village, while a sister, who married a Richardson, was the mother of Dr. A. P. Richardson, long a prominent physician of Walpole and one of Lempster's many able natives.

William B. Parker and his wife had three sons and two daughters. The oldest son, Alonzo, went to Boston, in early life and engaged in the market business. The second son, Sylvester A., taught penmanship in youth, fitted for college at the Green Mountain Liberal Institute, Woodstock, Vt., took a partial course at Tufts College, studied for the ministry and held several Universalist pastorates in Vermont, the last and largest at Bethel. The youngest son, Andrew, remained at home and became a farmer. Maria, the eldest daughter, married one Altamont Thompson, and after his death, became the wife of his brother, Horatio, both Lempster men; while the youngest daughter, Claribel, married Henry E. Huntley also of Lempster.

The second daughter of "Uncle Ames" Miner, Emma Eliza, married William Spaulding, a native of the town, and a brother of the late Rev. Willard Spaulding, D. D., an eloquent preacher of the Universalist denomination; by the way, it may as well be stated here as anywhere that Lempster claims the distinction of having reared more Universalist ministers than any other town in the country.

William Spaulding was a man of strong character and fine intellectual equipment, and had he been liberally educated, would have been an ornament to any profession. He lived on a farm on the Marlow road, the home being near the district school house. They had one child, a son, William Waldemar, generally known by the latter name, who was given a good education, graduating from Tufts College in 1867, of which institution he has been a trustee for more than forty years. He was a high school principal for fourteen years, after graduation, serving first in Adams, Mass., and later in Haverhill in the same state, where has been his residence ever since, and where he was for a number of years chairman of the school board. Relinquishing his work as a teacher he engaged in shoe manufacturing, which he followed successfully for nearly thirty years, and has since been engaged in banking, and incidentally for a time in cotton manufacturing at Easthampton, Mass. He is a director of the Citizens' Cooperative Bank of Haverhill, of the Morris Plan Institution, and of the First National Bank of Haverhill, and is President of the Haverhill Savings Bank, and may safely be accounted one of the most successful sons of Lempster from a business point of view. He sticks to his Republicanism in politics, and his Universalist religious faith, in which he was reared, and has long been accounted a "pillar" in the Universalist Church of Haverhill. He married Evelyn Alcie Harris of Oakdale, Mass. They have a son, a daughter and various grandchildren.

Rachel, the third daughter of Ames Miner, married one Edwin A. Tenney. They lived for a time while I was in Lempster, in a house midway between the Parker and Spaulding places, near the fork of the road leading to the "Street", but subsequently removed to La Crosse, Wis., where Mr. Tenney was engaged in the hardware business till his death many years ago, his wife surviving for some time. They had no children.

Fanny Miner, the fourth of the daughters, married Charles Booth. They lived for some time at the Miner family homestead, with her father and mother, but, later removed to South Boston, where both died many years ago. They had one son, Clarence, who died in boyhood.

It may be proper to note here, that William Spaulding and wife, and Charles Booth and wife, for some time constituted the choir at the Universalist church at "The Pond", which they, along with their father Miner, were instrumental in establishing and supporting.

Having referred to "Uncle Ames" Miner and his family, constituting an important group of people in School District No. 7, I shall mention in brief some of the other residents of the district. On the Marlow road, to the south of William B. Parker's, the next residence was that of Willard Rogers who had a son named Orvel, one of the "big boys" in the school during the first winter of my attendance. This son became a resident of Keene, and I met him some twenty-five years ago where he was employed in one of the wood-working establishments of that city. The Rogers home disappeared long since, through fire or otherwise.

Next below the Rogers place, and on the opposite side of the road was the home of one Harvey Huntley and family. He had a son, Henry, and two daughters, Olive and Minerva. Henry married Claribel Parker, as I have heretofore noted. Olive married Arvin Baker, who died some years ago, but she still lives, her home being in Marlow. She was in attendance, and read a selection at the last Old Home Day meeting in Lempster. The younger daughter, Minerva, married William Gee. Both are now dead.

In, off the road, to the right below the Huntley place, were two houses occupied by two brothers named Metcalf, Joseph and Jeremiah. Although doubtless descended from the original immigrant of the name, Michael of Dedham, Mass., (1637) as are most of the name in the country, they were not near relatives of my father. Jeremiah had no children, but Joseph had two sons, Alden E., and Solon, both of whom attended school during my own attendance. What became of these boys, I am unable to say, but they have doubtless "passed on", as well as their parents, long since.

Farther down the road towards Marlow, and in the last house in the district, according to my recollection, lived a brother and sister named Honey, both single and thoroughly devoted to each other. They were industrious and frugal people, carefully saving their earnings from year to year.

They subsequently removed to the farm, which had been occupied by O. S. Carey, where they lived several years, and later bought the Hiram Fletcher farm in the Dodge Hollow District, one of the best in town, where they continued to prosper. The brother's name was Duren and the sister was called Eliza. The former was a great reader, a fine scholar and a very eloquent speaker, as I distinctly remember, he having been Superintending School Committee for the town at one time, while I was attending the No. 7 school, which he visited. The brother and sister were both devoted Universalists, the former often officiating as a lay reader at the services in the little Universalist church, at "The Pond". After his decease, followed by that of his sister, it became evident what was the purpose of their thrifty, economical and saving life. All their property, to the value of about $20,000, was left to the Universalist State Convention, the income from the same to be expended in carrying on the work of the denomination in the state, and constitutes the basis of the permanent fund which the convention now holds.

On a road leading off the main road to Marlow, a little below the Parker place, and skirting the base of the mountain, lived two families within the limits of the district, one William Gee being the head of the first, and Jesse Hill of the other. There were four children in the Gee family— Horace, Harriet, Silas and William, though the latter was not of school age at the time of our removal to Lempster. Horace remained on the home farm; while Silas married the widow of Jeremiah Metcalf.

In the Hill family were a son and daughter— Leander and Rosette. Leander became a resident of the town of Langdon, where I presume he died. If Rosette married I am unable to say who was her husband, though I met her a few years since at an Old Home Day gathering, and I understand that she is now living in the "Old

Ladies' Home," in Newport.

Running off the Marlow road to the left, as we go north, just below the No. 7 school house, is the "old road" to the "Street." A short distance up this road lived two families, those of William Chappell and Alpheus Honey. The Chappells had no children, as I recall it, certainly none attending school, and they either died or moved away not long after our removal from Lempster, and the place passed into the hands of a Gordon family. Alpheus Honey was a brother of Duren S., heretofore mentioned. He had a small farm, well tilled, and a son and daughter—Alden and Orpha, who attended the school in my day. Later on, by a second wife, he had a younger daughter, Flora. Alden died comparatively early. Orpha was the second wife of Alfred J. Gould of Newport, and the mother of Mary A. Gould now residing there. Flora married a man named Smith and lived in Manchester, where she died many years ago.

Near the fork of the road, next beyond the school, lived Oliver Newell and wife, with no children, at home at least, and it is my impression that they had none; but Oliver had a mind of his own and did not hesitate to express it when occasion required. Running off to the south-east from the main highway, near the Newell place, was a road passing up over the side of the mountain. On this road, before the mountain was reached, were two farms, the one occupied by the family of Jacob B. Richardson and the other by that of Timothy Bruce. Mr. Richardson was a prominent citizen of the town, a leading Democrat, and had been a member of the board of selectmen, and a representative in the State Legislature. He had a family of three sons and a daughter. The sons were named J. Foster, Edmund B., and Truman, and the daughter, Olive, the latter being next older than Truman, the youngest son. All of these attended the district school, during the first winter of my attendance, but the two older sons not after that. My impression is that both these older sons were engaged for a time as traveling salesmen for Boston firms, but they were both in trade for themselves later in life, Foster at South Acworth and Edmund at Lempster Street. Both were married, the former twice, though I do not recall the names of his wives. Edmund married Elizabeth, a daughter of Alfred Ward of Croydon, whom I have mentioned as a resident of the old union school district in which I was born. I distinctly remember her as a school mate of mine during my two terms in that school, and as a decidedly handsome girl. These men and their wives passed away long since. Olive Richardson was a bright girl and became a successful school teacher. She finally married one George F. Nichols of South Acworth, with whom she became acquainted after her father's removal to that place, where he was for some years in business as a general merchant, before his decease. Nichols and his wife removed to Keene, where both died some time since. Truman Richardson, the younger son, married Ann Gowen of South Acworth and removed to Vermont, where he was engaged in farming at or near Chester. I met him a few years ago at an Old Home Day gathering in Acworth and have recently heard that he is still living in Chester. If so he must be an old man, as he was about two years my senior.

There were several sons and at least two daughters in the Bruce family, though I knew only the younger of the latter. The older sister, I think, married a man named Porter and lived at "The Pond." Ruth, the younger daughter, attended the winter school, while I was there, as did three of the sons, at least, during the first winter, John, Elisha and George. Timothy, Jr., an older son, had passed school age. Ruth subsequently married Emerson Hurd of Lempster, and they removed to Massachusetts, where I think, John and Elisha had also gone. George lost his life in the Union service during the Civil war.

Back from the road, near the Bruce place, lived a man named Jennings, concerning whom I only remember that he had a daughter, Martha, who attended the school, while a short distance up the mountain resided a family named Calkins, with a daughter, Ellen, in school during the first summer of my attendance, who, in my boyish fancy, was the handsomest girl I had ever seen. What became of her, or the rest of the family, I never knew.

A road leading off from the main highway, to the left and northward, beyond Oliver Newell's, brought one into quite a neighborhood of families, making an important part of the population of District No. 7, not all of whom I am able to recall at this time, but I remember that the first house reached, which was on the right hand side, was that of one Otis Field who had a daughter, Letitia, who was about my age and was a member of the school during my attendance. Subsequently she became the wife of Horace Gee, before mentioned. Mr. Field had two sons who had grown up and left home before our arrival in town, but whom I afterwards knew. These were Artemas C., who became a teacher and preacher, and George B., a mechanic, who resided for many years in South Acworth.

There was a Cutler family living just above, on the other side, who had a son, Lewis, who was one of the older boys in school in the winter. Subsequently, when I set out to teach school myself, I bought a silver watch of him, for the then substantial sum of ten dollars. This Lewis Cutler remained on the home place, married and reared several children, some of whom are now living.

Not far above lived Lewis Allen, who, in addition to a little farming, did a good business as a shoemaker. I recall that the first and only pair of long legged calf-skin boots that I ever had were made by him, and they were a good article—all for the modest sum of $4.00. Near the Allens lived Oliver Davis, with a number of sons in the school, of whom I remember Henry, Jefferson and Charles. I think Jefferson became a Methodist minister, but died young, and that none survived many years. I have the impression that one lost his life in the Civil War.

Off from the road for a distance, in a sightly location, was the "Perley place," so called, where was a fine farm and a pleasant home. There two successive generations of the family, most of whose members became prominent were reared. The original proprietor, Edmund Perley, had several daughters, and one son who grew to maturity. Abigail, the oldest daughter, the child of a first wife who died soon after her birth, married Gordon Way of Lempster, and was the mother of Dr. Osman B. Way and Mrs. Ira Colby of Claremont. Emily, the second daughter, was the wife of Peter T. Fox of Marlow and mother of Perley E. Fox, now living in that town, at the age of 92 years, and who is the oldest living past master of a subordinate Grange in the State.

Mehitable became the wife of Osman C. Baker, a native of Marlow, who started out as a teacher, but finally entered the Methodist ministry, and became a noted bishop of that church. Mrs. Osma C. Morrill, the talented musician of Concord, and a member of the Concord Board of Education, is their daughter. Maria married Rev. Alonzo A. Miner, the noted Universalist clergyman of Boston. Louisa was the wife of Joseph Swasey, prominent in railway circles in his day. Marietta married the Rev. Leon .C. Field, an eminent Methodist clergyman, prominent in the N. H. Conference; while Orpha C. the youngest, who was living at the old home, with her brother Asbury F., the only surviving son, at the time of our removal to Lempster subsequently married a man named Fales.

Ashbury F. Perley was a good farmer, a highly reputable citizen and a loyal supporter of the Methodist Church at "The Pond". He had one son and four daughters, none of school age while we lived in town. The son, George E., was a promising youth, and his life has well fulfilled the promise of early days. He graduated from Dartmouth College in the class of 1878; was for some time principal of the Charlestown high school; studied law with Hon. Ira Colby of Claremont, was admitted to the bar in 1883, and in the following years removed to Moorhead, Minn., where he has since been located in the practice of his profession, and in the conduct of an extensive Farm Loan Agency. He has been prominent in public affairs, serving as a member of the City government and the State Legislature, also for many years on the Moorhead Board of Education, and as a trustee of Fargo College, across the river in Fargo, S. D., wherein his younger sister, Mary Elizabeth, a highly educated woman was for nearly twenty years professor of German. Of his older sisters, two, Maria and Louise, were twins, bright, handsome and well educated. Maria married Freeman Gordon and resided in Enfield till her decease some years ago; while Louise became the wife of the late Dr. Ira Adams of Derry, where she still resides, but usually attends the Old Home gatherings in Lempster, where I once met her brother over twenty years ago. The other sister, Jennie, married the late Judge Corson, once prominent as a promoter, and is now residing in Chicago as is her sister, Mary Elizabeth, who has retired from her college work, and is now teaching in the "Windy City". Both of these younger women have been present at the Old Home gatherings in Lempster the last two years. A younger son of Asbury Perley died in youth, just as he was entering upon professional studies.

Other residents of the district, living in the Perley neighborhood were George W. Bryant, who had a son and daughter of school age, and

John Wheeler. The latter subsequently removed to Cambridge Hollow, or "Keyes", as the place is now called, where he engaged extensively in lumber manufacture. He was a man of much musical talent, as is his son, John, who succeeded him, and is still living at Keyes, while his wife, L. May Wheeler, has long been prominent in Grange work in Sullivan County.

Having mentioned, somewhat in detail, the various families that I call to mind, making up the most of the population of School District, No. 7, in Lempster, wherein our family resided for five years, from April 1852 to April 1857, it may be well now to speak of the school itself and my attendance in the same.

The summer term of 1852, the first which I attended, was under the instruction of Miss Mary Ann Nichols, an experienced teacher of that day, a native of the town and a member of a prominent family, two of whose brothers, Dennison and Orison Nichols, I recall as prosperous farmers of the town. She was a good disciplinarian and a thorough instructor, and the thirty or more pupils whom she had in charge held her in high esteem if not in affectionate regard. She was generally regarded as "strong minded", and wore what was then known as the "Bloomer" costume, which excited more remarks then than it would at the present day. She subsequently became the wife of one William T. Thissell, a young farmer living in the mountain region in the north-east part of the town, near her own old home, but survived her marriage only a few years.

The teacher the following winter was one Nathan R. Morse of Stoddard. He was a young man of exceptional ability and great force of character, and made a stronger impression upon my own mind and character than any teacher I had known up to that time. Politically he was a Democrat and in religion a Universalist and occasionally dropped remarks that indicated his sentiments in these regards. He had been fitting for college at Tubbs Union Academy in Washington, and entered Amherst in the succeeding autumn, from which he graduated in due course. I never saw him after he entered college till many years later, when I was editing the People and Patriot in Concord, and he was Governor of the New England order of the Pilgrim Fathers, and came there to attend a meeting of the order in his official capacity, and called on me during his stay. He was long a leading physician in the city of Salem, Mass., and chairman of the Democratic city committee, but died many years ago.

The school during the second summer of my attendance was taught by Miss Lima Hurd, a daughter of Collins Hurd (if I remember his name aright) who lived in town, some two miles up the road toward Goshen, (Mill Village), was a prosperous farmer and a "pillar" of the Methodist Church at "The Pond". Miss Hurd was also an experienced teacher and a very beautiful and amiable young woman, and was greatly beloved by the entire school. She ultimately married a man named Ober (I think) and went west, but died a few years later.

In the following winter, one George S. Thompson had charge of the school. Some of the older scholars of former winters were no longer in attendance, but younger ones came in so that the attendance remained about the same. Mr. Thompson was a Lempster boy and a good teacher very generally liked. He had a brother, Altamont, who was also a teacher, who married Maria Parker of this school, as previously noted, also a brother, Horatio, who succeeded him as her husband. Sullivan Thompson, married and settled in Claremont where he was a prominent citizen and an active supporter of the Universalist church for years.

My third and last summer term of school in Lempster was under the instruction of a young lady named Helen Chase, from the town of Washington. She was a good teacher and enjoyed her work, and as it was to be my last summer in school I endeavored to make the best of my opportunity during the term. Miss Chase was the daughter of Hon. Martin Chase of Washington, a leading Democrat of the town and for some years Judge of the Common Pleas Court. She never married and, later in life, lived for many years with relatives in the town of Marlboro in this state, where I met her a dozen years ago, or more, while attending a Universalist state convention in that town. Some two years ago I heard, incidentally, that she was living in an Invalids' Home, in the city of Keene, and wrote her there, receiving in reply a long, interesting and exceedingly well written letter, though I believe she was then in her 90th year. She was the last survivor of my teachers, and but a few days since I learned of her decease in Keene, at the age of 91.

In the following winter, that of 1854-5 one Thomas T. Smith taught the school. Whether it was my fault or his I know not, but I am sure that he made less impression upon my mind than any other teacher that I ever had. I think his home was in Unity, but what he ever did in life, or what became of him, I never knew.

During the next winter the school was in charge of a woman, the first female teacher for a winter term in the district. Her name was Nancy Marion Green, and her home was in Barnard, Vermont. It happened that Sylvester A. Parker had been attending the Green Mountain Liberal Institute, at South Woodstock, where he met Miss Green, to whom he had become engaged, and through some family influence with the prudential committee she had been hired to come down into the Parker neighborhood in Lempster, and teach the school, thus making it pleasant for two people at least. I soon arrived at the conclusion that teaching was only an incident with her that winter, and cut short my attendance, whether foolishly or otherwise. She soon after married Mr. Parker, but died quite early in life, and he married again.

In the following winter, 1856-7, the school had another female teacher, but of a different type. This was Olive L. Richardson, whom I have previously mentioned as a daughter of Jacob B. Richardson, a resident of the district, who had already taught one or two summer terms elsewhere, with much success, and whose engagement for this winter service here was generally satisfactory. She was in love, but only with her work, and she made all the scholars, old and young, love her also. Subsequently, after her family's removal to South Acworth she married George F. Nichols of that place and they made their home in Keene, till death.

In the fall of 1856, preceeding this last winter term in Lempster, I had persuaded my father to let me attend a term of select school, taught at "The Street" by Miss Dency Hurd, a very competent teacher of much experience. The distance from our house was three miles which I traveled each way daily, regardless of weather, glad of the opportunity, and applied myself to my studies as zealously as possible, and made as good progress as could reasonably be expected, although there was a good deal of political excitement at the time, it being in the midst of the Buchanan and Fremont campaign, and I had begun to take a deep interest in partisan questions. Several political meetings were held in the hall, below the school room, during the campaign, which I managed to attend. Among the speakers, on the Democratic side were Hon. Henry Hubbard of Charlestown, a former Governor and United States Senator and Anson S. Marshall of Concord, then a young lawyer, but a brilliant speaker. The only Republican speaker, whose name I recall, was Mason W. Tappan of Bradford, afterwards a member of Congress and Attorney General of the State, who, by the way, was a native of Newport.

After school hours many of the older scholars used to linger on the steps and engage in somewhat heated political discussion. I was on the Democratic side of course, along with two or three bright girls. These were Georgianna Carey, who afterward became the wife of Dr. S. M. Dinsmoor of Keene; Louise Huntoon, subsequently Mrs. George E. Dame, and Louise Barnard, an Acworth girl, who later removed with her family to Minnisota. The Republican cause was championed by George E. Dame, who later became a Democrat, and was for some years

Clerk of Court for Sullivan County, and two Collins girls, Sarah and Mary, daughters of Deacon James Collins.

I still vividly recall the fact of having been made the victim of a boyish prank on one occasion during my attendance upon this term of school, which gave me the greatest fright of my life, though I have laughed over it many times since.

Some time during the day in question I overheard a group of boys talking, quite excitedly, as it seemed, about a large panther having been seen the day before, in the woods, south of the "Street," through which ran the road by which I came and went on my way to and from school. There was a long strip of woodland, of nearly a mile in extent, without a break, or a house on the way. It was quite late and beginning to grow dark when I started for home that afternoon, and soon after I entered the woods I was startled by an unearthly schreeching, apparently just over the ridge on the left hand side of the road. It was a real hair-lifting schreech, such as a full grown, hungry panther might be supposed to make, and I immediately recalled the conversation I had heard that day, and started upon a run down the road toward home, surpassing in speed anything in the line ever accomplished by me before or since, not abating the rate of progress till I was well out of the woods, on the final lap of my journey home.

The group of boys which I have mentioned, who put up this job or joke on me, included two or three sons of John Wilcox, who lived on the West road, running from the "Street" to Dodge Hollow, and Willard O. Hurd, a son of Henry Hurd, living nearby. Just which ones of these Wilcox boys were in this "job" I am now unable to say. The three older boys were William, John and George. A younger one Orion, was not old enough at the time to have been in it. William, John and Orion were subsequently residents of Michigan, but probably none of them are now living. It is a fact, that some Newport residents will remember, that peaches were at times received in the local market from the Wilcox Bros., of Michigan. George W. Wilcox, a prominent Grand Army veteran, was living at Long Beach, California, a few years ago, and made a visit to his native state.

With Willard Hurd I soon after became well acquainted, and we became close friends. He finally went to Carleton Place in Canada, where an older brother of his, William H. Hurd, was located in the practice of medicine, and studied with him for that profession, to the practice of which he ultimately devoted his life. We corresponded for some time while he was there, and a more interesting letter writer I have never known. He was in the Federal service for a time, during the Civil War, as a surgeon or assistant surgeon, and later engaged in the practice of his profession in the town of Grantham, where he remained for many years; but ultimately, in broken health, became an inmate of the N. H. Soldier's Home at Tilton, where he died some years since. His daughter, Anne, an accomplished young woman, now the wife of Fred C. Parker of Wilton, was for several years the Cataloger in the State Library at Concord, where she did most efficient work.

It may be noted that another older brother of Willard O. Hurd, Charles E., who was for a time a resident of Lempster, while the family were making their home there, became prominent in the literary and journalistic world. He was connected with newspapers in different parts of the country and was a writer of no mean order. For many years preceding his death he was the literary editor of the Boston Transcript, and his work gave that department of the paper a standing which it had never before attained.

In referring to various residents of School district No. 7, in which we resided in Lempster, mention was made of Duren Honey, and his service as Superintending School Committee, which office he held for a year or two after our removal there, and which he filled most acceptably, taking great interest in the schools, which he visited frequently, interestingly addressing the scholars.

The successor of Mr. Honey in this office was Lucius A. Spencer, generally known as Austin from his middle name. Mr. Spencer, who was the son of Ralph Spencer, a thrifty farmer and prominent citizen residing in the mountain district, was himself a good scholar, much interested in educational work, and looked closely after the welfare of the schools. He subsequently studied for the ministry and became a Universalist preacher, but had not fairly settled in his work when the Civil War broke out, and he enlisted in the Union service, in which he finally lost his life.

The next incumbent of the Superintendent's office, serving the last year of my residence and school attendance in No. 7, was Hon. Daniel M. Smith, one of the town's most prominent citizens, and long time leader of the Democratic party, in which capacity he found himself pitted against another Smith, generally known as Deacon Alvah Smith, who was for many years the head and front of the Republican party in town, though for some time, in the later years of his life, he posed as a Prohibitionist and Labor Reformer. There were heated political contests in those days, though the Democrats were generally successful, and the two Smiths were looked to for leadership by their respective parties.

Daniel M. Smith was a farmer living in the central northern part of the town; while Alvah was a tanner, located at the "Street." Daniel M., was affiliated with the Methodist Church at the "Pond," while Alvah was the "high light" in the Congregational church at the "Street." In the absence of a lawyer in town, each of these men did considerable business in the capacity of a justice of the peace. If a Republican got in trouble he was sure to consult Deacon Alvah, and if a Democrat was in difficulty he ordinarily depended upon Daniel M. to help him out. In this way, aside from their political antagonism, a strong spirit of rivalry was engendered between the two, and their respective partisans were generally ready to follow their lead. The families of both these men are extinct so far as Lempster is concerned, though both had considerable families. That of Daniel M. consisted mainly of daughters, as I recall. Whether any of them are living, or not, I am unable to say, but it occurs to me that one of them was the mother of Mrs Vincent J. Brennan, Sr., of Newport.

Among other prominent citizens of Lempster were Alden and William B. Sabin, Deacon James H. Collins, Alden Carey and Ashbury F. Perley (the latter of whom was mentioned among District No. 7 residents) on the Republican side, and Ramson P. Beckwith, Hiram and Hosea W. Parker, Olivet S. Carey (generally known as Saxon) and William B. Parker and Jacob B. Richardson, before mentioned as District No. 7 residents, on the Democratic; all of whom were to be depended upon for good work in their respective party causes. Ransom P. Beckwith was a man of character and ability, modest and unassuming, but trusted and honored by his fellow citizens, whom he served frequently as selectman, and represented in the legislature. His wife, who survived him for many years was a daughter of the late Benjamin Parker, and a sister of Hiram and Hosea W. They had two sons, Walter P., and Hira. The former graduated from Tufts College and became a successful teacher. He was for some years before his death principal of the Salem, Mass., Normal School, at a time when it was noted that of the nine Normal Schools in that State, seven had New Hampshire men as principals. Hira, the younger son, has long been a prominent citizen of Claremont, and one of the most successful architects in Western New Hampshire.

The Parker brothers, Hiram and Hosea W., were among the most promising young men in town, in the days of my residence in Lempster. Their father, Benjamin Parker, had died before they had reached their majority, leaving the care of the farm and the maintenance of the home with their mother, in their hands. They bravely accepted the situation and devoted their energies to the work in hand. After a time, however; Hosea W. developed an ambition for a professional career. Whether from choice or a sense of duty, or both, Hiram decided to stick to the old homestead, and did so for many years, caring for his mother and rearing a family of his own. He married Helen G. Moore, a Lempster girl, daughter of Charles Moore who lived in the north part of the town. (There were two men named Charles Moore, by the way, living in Lempster, generally known as "North Charles" and "South Charles.") They had three children, two sons, Fred C. and Carl A. and one daughter, Jennie L., who married the late H. F. Olmstead, and has lately resided in Lancaster.

After carrying on the farm successfully till middle life Hiram Parker bought the old Abner Chase stand at the Street, and there conducted a general store until about six years ago when he sold out and went with his son, Carl A., to Penacook, where the latter had purchased a clothing and shoe store, where he remained until his death late in 1924. While in Lempster Mr. Parker served the town repeatedly in all offices within its gift, as selectman, town clerk, moderator and representative, being the oldest surviving member of the House of Representatives in the state at the time of his death, having served in that body in 1863 and 1864, or 60 years previous. He also served as postmaster of Lempster for 24 years, from 1889, and was a delegate in the Constitutional Convention of 1912. From 1875 to

1887 he was the Sullivan County member of the N. H. Board of Agriculture. His oldest son, Fred C., who married Anne Hurd, previously referred to, who was graduated from the New Hampshire College in 1879, was engaged in mercantile business in Acworth for several years; subsequently was for some time a traveling salesman, and later in business at Lancaster from which, as I have recently learned he has just retired, and will make his home in the town of Wilton.

Hosea W. Parker, the younger brother, fitted for college at Tubbs Union Academy in Washington, and the Green Mountain Liberal Institute at South Woodstock, Vt., took a partial course at Tufts, studied law with Hon. Edmund Burke of Newport, was admitted to the bar in 1859, and commenced practice in Claremont in 1860, where he continued until his death in the summer of 1922, in his 90th year. In his early life, while securing his education and studying his profession, he was a very successful teacher in winter in the district schools of the County, and was engaged one winter, while reading law in Mr. Burke's office, in the north village district in Newport, as some of the old residents may possibly remember. About this time, he served as Superintending Committee in Lempster, where he held his residence, and which town he represented in the State Legislature, in 1859 and 1860.

Hosea W. Parker was an ardent Democrat and

zealous Universalist. He served his party, and the country, in Congress from 1871 to 1875; was many years President of the Universalist State Convention, and twice elected President of the Universalist General Convention. He was for many years counsel for the town of Claremont, was prominent in educational affairs, as a trustee of the High School, and moderator of the District; he also served as a member of the last Constitutional Convention, and was temporary chairman at the organization of that body. At the time of his death he was the oldest Sunday School Superintendent in the country, as well as the oldest member of the Sullivan County Bar, of which he had long been President. He was also for many years a trustee of Tufts College from which he received the honorary degree of L. L. D. in 1912. He married in 1861, Caroline Lovisa Southgate, who died in 1904. Their daughter, Lizzie L. (Smith College 1888) is the wife of Lee S. McCollester, D. D., dean of Tufts College Divinity School.

Lempster has sent out many men who have been prominent in different lines of activity, in other places. Recent reference was made to Hosea W. Parker, eminent lawyer and leading citizen of Claremont. Another lawyer, previously mentioned, who went out from Lempster, is George E. Perley of Moosehead, Minn., still active in business there, while still another son of the town became prominent in the legal profession and the public service of the latter state, in the person of Anson L. Keyes, a son of Orison Keyes, a resident of what was formerly known as "Cambridge Hollow," in the north-west part of the town, on the Acworth border, but has latterly been called "Keyes," on account of the manufacturing activities carried on there by Mr. Keyes and his younger sons, Martin L. and Frank E., of whom the former later engaged in business in Maine and the latter in California. Anson L. Keyes was a Dartmouth College graduate of the class of 1872, and of the Albany Law School of the following year. He located in practice in Faribault, Minn., where he attained success in his profession, serving as city solicitor and solicitor for Rice County, and also as attorney for the Rock Island and Pacific R. R. He was also interested in educational affairs, and was many years a member of the Faribault board of education. He died several years ago, leaving a wife and daughter.

More physicians than lawyers, however, went out from Lempster. We have mentioned Drs. William H. and Willard O. Hurd, sons of Henry Hurd; but there was another Hurd family, long prominent in town, one member of which became prominent in the medical profession. This was the family of Smith Hurd, a grandson of Shubael Hurd, one of the town's first settlers. One of the sons, George W., remained on the home farm, where he also was succeeded by his son, Elbert E., whose death was recently announced. Yorick, the elder son of Smith Hurd, was the physician just spoken of. He graduated from the Dartmouth Medical School and commenced practice in Amesbury, Mass., but soon removed to Ipswich, where he was quite successful, and was for many years in charge of the Essex County House of Correction. Another Dartmouth Medical graduate, born in Lempster, was Dr. Abel P. Richardson, who was a prominent practitioner in the town of Walpole for more than a third of a century, previous to his death in 1900.

Carl A. Allen, previously mentioned as having been born at the base of the mountain near the shore of Sand Pond (now Echo Lake), was graduated from the Long Island College Hospital in 1874, after a course in the Bowdoin College Medical School. He commenced practice in Acworth, where he remained till 1890, serving meanwhile for ten years as Superintendent of School, an office which he had previously filled for two years in Lempster. Removing to Holyoke, Mass., he soon gained high standing in the profession there; was a member of the Connecticut Valley, Massachusetts and American Medical Societies, also President of the Holyoke Medical Association, the Hampden County Medical Society and the Holyoke Association for the Prevention and

Relief of Tuberculosis. To the work of the latter organization he was particularly devoted during the closing years of his life, which came to an end some four years since.

Another Lempster born physician of high standing in his profession, and still in active practice is Dr. Abram W. Mitchell, son of Andrew J. Mitchell. Dr. Mitchell graduated from the Medical College of the University of New York in 1887, practiced a year in the town of Harrisville and then removed to Epping, where he has since been located. Another son of Lempster who gained much success in the medical profession was Dr. Osmon B. Way, who was born March 22, 1849, educated at Kimball Union Academy and Dartmouth Medical College, from which he graduated in 1865, and immediately commenced practice at South Acworth, where he remained two years and then removed to Claremont. He gained a wide practice there and was active in public affairs, serving at one time in the State Legislature. He died about ten years ago.

Reference to physicians who have gone out from Lempster, may well be followed by allusion to sons of Lempster who have pursued the practice of dentistry, which is closely allied with that of medicine. Three of these, all of whom I knew well in the early days, were reared in the same school district, generally known as the "Dodge

Hollow" district, wherein were located a saw and grist mill on Dodge brook, which has its rise in Dodge Pond, from which the "Pond" village takes its name, and flows circuitously through the southern part of the town. These three dentists were Ozias M. George, Levi C. Taylor and Charles A. Brackett. Dr. George studied dentistry with several experienced practitioners and located in practice at Bellows Falls, Vt., where he continued through life, with much success in his profession, and was also engaged in various outside business enterprises, aside from serving in the Vermont legislature and in other public capacities. He had a daughter, who became the wife of Charles H. Robb, former Assistant Attorney General of the United States and, later, an Associate Justice of the District of Columbia Supreme Court of Appeals. He was a son of Nathan George, one of the best farmers in town, whose oldest son, Frank, was also in business in Bellows Falls, as proprietor of the railway restaurant, while a younger one, Alanson B., located on a farm in the northeastern part of Lempster, where he still resides.

Dr. Levi C. Taylor was the son of Erastus Taylor, who was also a good farmer, and a son of Deacon John Taylor, who was a "pillar" of the Congregational church at the "Street." It is historically recorded that John Taylor had the contract to remove the old first church edifice, which was located on the hill, midway between the "Pond" and the "Street", which was done in 1822, and an imposing belfry and steeple added. This old church building, which was abandoned for church purposes in 1835, when a new church was erected, was occupied as a town hall for many years, until about 1858, when the present town hall at the "Pond" was erected. It is still owned by the town, the lower hall being used for various public gatherings, and the Grange having quarters above, where formerly select schools were held in the spring and autumn for many years. Dr. Taylor, worked on his father's farm till he attained his majority, and worked well, as we have occasion to know, as his father and mine occasionally "changed work", as was a frequent custom among neighborhood farmers in those days, and Levi and I went along with our fathers in the process, and I had more than one hard day's work in keeping Levi busy with a shovel or hoe. On coming of age he left home, with five dollars in his pocket, to make his way in the world, which he did with ultimate success. getting a little schooling at Henniker Academy and then entering the office of Dr. George Bowers of Springfield, Vt., to learn the dental profession. After two years of hard application he commenced practice at Holyoke, Mass., but two years later removed to Hartford, Conn., where he continued through life. He was not only a thorough practitioner, but a close student, following all lines of progress in his profession. He was a member of various dental societies, and lectured extensively before dental organizations. He was a lecturer on oral prophylaxis and orthodontia, in the New York College of Dental and Oral Surgery, for a number of years. He died several years since, leaving a wife, who was Miss Nellie Thayer of Peterboro, and a daughter, Maude W., a practicing physician of Hartford, two sons having passed away.

The third of the dentists referred to, Dr. Charles A. Brackett, is the son of the late Joseph Brackett of the same district, but who removed during the son's early life to Acworth, where, as in Lempster, he was a successful farmer. Charles A. was a delicate boy, unfitted for manual labor, but was a fine scholar and made the best of such educational advantages as were at hand, and at twenty years of age entered the office of Dr. Taylor, before mentioned, who was several years his senior, as a student in dentistry, continuing three years, but in the meantime pursuing a course in the Harvard University Dental School from which he graduated in 1873. He located in practice in Newport, R. I., soon attaining a wide clintele among the aristocratic residents of that famous resort, and achieving remarkable success. He was a teacher in the Harvard Dental school, as instructor, assistant professor and professor, for half a century; has been prominent in many dental organizations, serving as President of the American Academy of Dental Science, and as a delegate to the International Medical Congress on several occasions. He has also been actively prominent in civic affairs in Newport, in which he still takes great interest, although retired from professional service. No son of Lempster has won greater distinction than Dr. Brackett, and none has been more loyal to his native town, which he has often visited on Old Home Day, as was the case, it should be said, of Dr. Taylor as well.

Lempster has produced a number of clergymen, mostly of the Universalist denomination, of whom there have been six or eight, or more, it is said, than have been born in any other town in the country; but the more prominent of these have already incidentally been mentioned, Rev. Dr. A. A. Miner having been the most distinguished and Rev. Dr. Willard Spaulding also quite noted, as was Rev. Sylvester A. Parker. Rev. Homer Taylor Fuller, D. D., L. L. D., was an ordained clergyman of the Congregational denomination, and for a time successfully held a pastorate in Wisconsin, but he was generally known as an educator, having devoted most of his life to that work. He was the son of Sylvanus and Sarah M. (Taylor) Fuller, born November 15, 1838. I had slight acquaintance with him in youth when he was known as the best scholar in town. He fitted for college at Kimball Union Academy, Meriden (which school, by the way, has fitted more men for college who have gained distinction in public and professional life than any other in the country) and graduated from Dartmouth in the class of 1864.

Dr. Fuller was for three years principal of the Fredonia, N. Y. Academy immediately after graduation, and before studying for the ministry, for which he fitted at the Andover and Union Theological Seminaries. Resuming educational work he was for a time principal of St. Johnsbury, Vt., Academy, and for twelve years President of the Worcester, Mass., Polytechnic Institute, retiring in 1894 to become President of Drury College, Missouri, which position he occupied till 1905. He received the degree of Ph. D. from Dartmouth in 1880; D. D., from Iowa College in 1898, and L. L. D., from Drury in 1905. Retiring from active labor he returned to Fredonia, N. Y., and died some years later at Saranac Lake.

We have already referred to Walter P. Beckwith, another successful educator, native of the town, some time principal of the Salem, Mass., Normal School, who died in the prime of manhood, and should have mentioned the fact that the Rev. Dr. Miner, whose chief distinction was that of a great preacher served for twelve years as President of Tufts College, was an overseer of Harvard University, and was a member of the Massachusetts State Board of Education for a longer time than any other man up to that day.

Another son of Lempster, who spent the greater part of his life in teaching, was Daniel B. Wheeler, who after several years service in that line in different places, was for fifteen years principal of the Shepard School in Cambridge, Mass. Retiring he returned to his old home in Lempster, but continued his interest in school affairs and served for several years as Commissioner of Education for Sullivan County. His son, Bertrand T. Wheeler, also a native of Lempster, who graduated from Dartmouth in 1884, has attained distinction as a Civil engineer, and has been chief engineer for the Maine Central Railroad for many years past.

Among daughters of Lempster who have done excellent educational work was Eliza, daughter of Abner Chase, who taught successfully for some years, and was for a time a member of the faculty of Tilton Seminary, with which her husband, Rev. C. S. Harrington, D. D., was officially connected. No Lempster born teacher, however, was ever more devoted to her work, or gained more fully the affectionate regard of her pupils than Dency Hurd, who had much experience as a district and select school teacher in Lempster and vicinity, who took a deep interest in the welfare of all of her scholars, and was unfailing in encouragement and advice. She was a daughter of Smith Hurd, of whom we have spoken, and married Lucius A. Spencer, who died soon after. Subsequently she married Espasi King, and removed to Vineland, N. J., where she died in 1882.

During the first year of my residence in Lempster I attended the Methodist Church at the "Pond", that being the church which my mother favored. If I remember aright the pastor of the church that year was one Rev. Lorenzo Draper, who had two daughters, one bright black-eyed one named Harriet, who probably attracted my attention more than did his sermons, which did not strongly impress me. At all events I concluded to go with my father, who was a Congregationalist, the next year, to the church of that denomination at the "Street".

The pastor of that church, at that time, was Rev. Robert Page, whose sermons were of the usual order of Congregational sermons of the day. These made no more impression on my mind than did those I heard in the Methodist Church the year before; but I had a new experience here, having been put into the Sunday School, when I was assigned to the class taught by Deacon Alvah Smith, made up of boys about my age, among whom I now recall Levi C. Taylor, whom I have heretofore mentioned as becoming a successful dentist, and George E. Dame, subsequently for many years clerk of Court for Sullivan County. Deacon Smith's admonitions were received as well meant, but their lasting effect may not have been as beneficial as he had hoped.

Early in the third year of our Lempster residence I broke away from parental restraint, as it were, and accepted the invitation of "Uncle Ames" Miner to attend the services at the little Universalist chapel at the "Pond". Although services were held here every Sunday, the society was able to hire a minister only one Sunday in four, some layman conducting the service for the balance of the time, there being several who acted in that capacity.

The preacher during the first year of my attendance was the Rev. Nathan R. Wright, a native of the town of Washington, who was also then residing there, though he had been settled in various other places as pastor. He was an able man and a good preacher, but his service in Lempster came to an end at the close of the first year of my attendance, he having been called to a pastorate in Massachusetts, in which state he spent the balance of his life. He was the father of Col. Carroll D. Wright, the eminent statistician, one time head of the U. S. Bureau of Labor.

The preacher the next year was the Rev.

Lemuel Willis of Warner, who was a man of solid attainments and exceptional ability. Although well advanced in years, having held many pastorates in this and other states, his sermons were always up-to-date, argumentative and convincing. He passed his last days in Warner, and the old Willis home has ever been held by his descendants. His son, Harlan, retained it, and the latter's son, Arthur L., of Concord, sometime Deputy Secretary of State, made it his summer home. Another son of Lemuel Willis, Algernon S., was long a prominent resident of Concord, as was his son, Eben.

Mr. Willis' service here was for a year only, when he was succeeded by the Rev. Joseph Barber of Alstead, another "old timer", who, although less brilliant than his predecessors, was a good preacher, and personally very well liked. Among the laymen who conducted services in the absence of a regular preacher were Hiram and Hosea W. Parker, Ransom P. Beckwith, Duren Honey and Lucius A. Spencer. Among those whom I recall as regular attendants upon the Universalist service were the Miners, Parkers, Spauldings, Beckwiths, Spencers, Pollards, Nicholses, Honeys, Huntoons, Careys, (Olivet S.) Richardsons, Cutlers and Georges. They were not a numerous company, but earnestly devoted to their church and its faith.

The people of Lempster, generally speaking,

in these days, were similar in character to the soil of the town—rugged and strong. Most of them gained their livelihood by tilling the soil, which yielded fair returns. There was comparatively little manufacturing. A saw and grist mill at Dodge Hollow, as before mentioned; another saw mill and the Keyes wood working establishment at Cambridge Hollow, where there was also, at an earlier day, some kind of a woolen mill operated by a man named Shepardson, and a small hand-rake factory in the northeastern part of the town, operated by the Alexanders, constituted everything in the manufacturing line in the town, aside from the tannery of Alvah Smith at the "Street", in connection with which he ran a large shoe factory for some years, which was destroyed by fire along with the tannery many years ago.

It was in this town and among these people that my own character and ambitions took shape, the years spent here being among the formative years of life, from eleven to sixteen years of age. For the people of Lempster, as I knew them then, and for such of them as I have known in later years I have always entertained a feeling of deep regard. They were good men and true women. For two of the latter I have always felt under deep obligation for the kindly interest that they manifested in my welfare, and the good advice which they gave me. These were Mrs. William

Spaulding (Emma Eliza Miner) and Dency Hurd, the teacher of whom I have heretofore spoken. They were noble women in the fullest sense of the term, and many a young person was benefitted from their acquaintance and friendship.

When, in the spring of 1857, my father purchased a larger and better farm, in the town of Acworth, to which the family, increased by the birth of two sons, removed, it was with some regret that I left the scenes with which I had become familiar, and the friends I had made in the five years of our residence in Lempster, but with bright hopes for the future, in a larger and more promising field of material activity, and a chance for new friendships and a wider acquaintance.

The farm to which we removed was located on the southern slope of Grout Hill, and was one of the best in that part of the town which was always regarded as a good farming town. The owner, from whom my father purchased it was one Lemuel Morse, but it had formerly been known as the Clark place. It embraced about 100 acres of land, of which forty acres were in mowing and tillage, mostly the former. It seemed to me there were many more acres before we got over it, the first summer, as my father and I cut all the grass by hand, mowing machines not being in vogue to much extent in those days, and I pitched on every load of the forty tons of hay, in which fact, as a boy of sixteen, I took considerable pride.

The outlook from this Acworth farm, especially from the house, which sat upon the crest of a knoll, was particularly fine, commanding as it did a view in the foreground across the valley of the Cold River, of the striking rock-crested elevation known as Gates Mountain, with wide reaches of romantic scenery on either side. From the window of my room I used frequently to look out upon this rocky summit in the early morning, as the first rays of the rising sun bathed it in golden splendor and the scene was, indeed, a most inspiring one. It awakened whatever of the poetic instinct I may have been endowed with, and often led me to the attempt, at least, to express myself in verse.

Here I passed the five years of my life, from 16 to 21. I was busily engaged most of the time in labor upon the farm, or in other work incident thereto, such as cutting and drawing wood and timber in the winter season. There was much to do and the labor was by no means easy, nearly all performed by hand, as was then generally the case. I did succeed, however, in getting the opportunity, for a few weeks in the autumn, for the first three years, 1857,'58 and '59, to attend select schools; the first year at Lempster Street, again, where Dency Hurd was still the teacher, and the second and third at South Acworth, then generally known as "Parks' Hollow", where Rev.

Artemas C. Field was the teacher one year and George R. Brown, then of Acworth, but later a Newport lawyer, the next.

My schoolmates at Lempster were about the same as during the previous autumn, except that Louise Huntoon and Georgianna Carey, who had been my active supporters in the political controversies carried on, were not in attendance, but some others not present the year before were in attendance at this term, of whom I recall particularly Eunice Hurd, a younger sister of Dency and herself a teacher, who was a very bright and handsome young woman, and one Sylvia Clark, a young lady from Derry, N. H., I believe, who was boarding for the term with the family of Deacon James H. Collins, whose bright daughters, Sarah and Mary, were again among the pupils. This Sylvia Clark, who was for sometime later a teacher, subsequently married. I do not recall her husband's name; but only a few years since I heard of her as living with a daughter in Springfield, Mass., or in that vicinity. Eunice Hurd died, unmarried, a few years later, greatly mourned by all who knew her.

At the fall term of school in South Acworth, in 1858, I attended only about six weeks, as Mr. Field, the teacher, who had at times operated as an "Evangelist", saw fit in the last half of the term to devote a part of the morning hour to religious instruction along a line which seemed unreasonable and preposterous to my mind. I therefore bade the school a regretful adieu, and returned to my old field of manual labor on the Grout Hill farm. I disliked to leave, on some accounts, however, not the least of which was the fact that Georgianna Carey and Louise Barnard, who had been in attendance with me at Miss Hurd's school at Lempster "Street" in 1856 and who were very pleasant and interesting school mates, were then attending the South Acworth school.

In the fall of 1859, when George R. Brown was the teacher, I attended the fall term, enjoyed it greatly and made the best of my opportunity. Mr. Brown, who had considerable experience as a teacher, took a deep interest in his work and sought to insure the interest of all his pupils, which he generally succeeded in doing. While most of the scholars in attendance resided in the immediate neighborhood, some came from a distance, and boarded in the village. Of these I remember in particular Miss Charlotte S. Wright, a daughter of Rev. Nathan R. Wright, to whom I have heretofore referred, then living, I believe, at Alstead, or "Paper Mill Village", and a Miss Emily Greene, whose home was also in Alstead.

Of the South Acworth scholars I recall George W. McDuffee, who subsequently became a prominent manufacturer in Keene, and Mayor of the city, and his sister, Martha J., who was the first young lady I ever escorted to an entertainment, and who subsequently married George B. Field, brother of the Rev. Artemas and son of Otis Field, mentioned as a resident of District No. 7, in Lempster. The Houston girls, Ellen and Mary, were among the best students in the school, and their cousin, Emily Boynton, who was living in their family at the time, was another of the same kind. She became a teacher and taught the Grout Hill school in the summer of 1860. Later she married a Gilsum man, named Mark, who many years after represented that town in the legislature and I met her in Concord while he was attending the session. The student most admired by the young men, however, was Minerva J. Adams, daughter of Nathan Adams, a woolen manufacturer, who had recently come in from the town of Washington. She was a charming girl, both in mind and person, and an accomplished musician, which fact enhanced her attractiveness. She had many admirers, but favored none of them, and died a few years since while a member of the family at the Centennial Home in Concord. Her brother, a few years younger, Irving W. Adams, was for many years burser of the Smithsonian Institute in Washington, D. C., where he died a year or two ago.

During this term of school a "Lyceum" was organized in South Acworth, holding weekly meetings in the school house, in which not only the older students, but many of the men and women of the village and vicinity, took part. Animated discussions were carried on; papers and essays read, and music and select readings enjoyed. Among the "outsiders" who were prominent in the discussions, were William F. Whitman, a mill man of the village, who had married Clara D., a daughter of Joel Porter, who subsequently became a practicing physician in Bellows Falls, and Newton, Mass., after her husband's death in the Civil War; James A. Wood, later prominent in Republican politics and the father of George A. Wood, now Speaker of the House of Representatives; his brother-in-law, J. Symonds Bowers, a brother of the late Hon. Shepard L. Bowers of Newport, and Orville Slader, subsequently proprietor of a large Boston restaurant. These were all good speakers and contributed largely to the interest of the Lyceum meetings. It should also be stated that Edward B. Smith, who subsequently practiced law at Paper Mill Village, and Ezra M. Smith, still practicing in Peterboro, at 88 years of age, being the oldest living member of the New Hampshire bar, used to come over from Alstead and take part in the debate. Mention of the South Acworth Lyceum of the fall of 1859, recalls the fact that there was a select school in session at that time at Acworth Center, or "The Town," as that villege was commonly called in distinction from South Acworth or "The Hollow," the teacher being one H. J. Crippen, who was subsequently in charge of a Western investment business in Concord for many years. It was given out at one time during the autumn, that Crippen and his older students were coming down to the "Hollow," on some Lyceum night to "do up" the South Acworthites in debate, or "otherwise." On a certain evening they entered the school room where the Lyceum was in session. They were courteously treated, and allowed to participate in the discussion of the question. Just what the question was, I do not remember, but I do remember that the debate was quite heated, the two teachers, Brown and Crippen, taking the prominent part, on opposite sides. I recall that one of the "Town" contingent was William Brooks, a son of Chapin K. Brooks, a merchant and prominent resident of the Center, and a younger brother of John Graham Brooks of Cambridge, Mass., the eminent sociologist and lecturer. This William Brooks was later associated with other Acworth natives in business in Holyoke, Mass., where he still resides, but retains so much interest in Acworth that he sends a check every year to pay the expense of an orchestra for Old Home Day music.

Recurring to the matter of the Lyceum contests, I am still of the impression that South

Acworth was not "done up" in the debate, and although there were some sharp words passed between the contending forces, outside the house after session ended, no blood was shed, no blows were struck and the dove of peace finally spread its wings over the scene.

Recurring to my farm labor experience on Grout Hill, I will mention one that I have never forgotten. It was a custom in that neighborhood for the farms to "change work" in haying. So it happened that on a particularly hot day Milon Cummings and I were at work with Milo Newton and Nathaniel P. Merrill, in the upper field on the Merrill place, Newton having married Hannah Merrill and taken charge of the farm. It was good land (as was most of the land on Grout Hill) and the grass crop was heavy. There were a number of acres in the field, and Newton, who was a strong, wiry man, "hard as nails," proposed it all be cut before dinner. He took the lead, Merrill, who was a year older than I came next, and Cummings and myself followed. Cummings was younger than myself, and had the rear position. We were young but ambitious, and did not propose to be outdone. So we worked beyond our strength, although refreshed occasionally by something a little stronger than the law allows at the present day, as was the universal custom in "haying time" in those days. Although the afternoon work was not as strenuous as that in the forenoon, we two youngsters were a tired lot, long before sundown, and neither ever forgot the experience of the day.

Speaking of Milon D. Cummings I might say that he was the youngest of eight children of Alvah and Polly (Grout) Cummings and one of a somewhat remarkable family. There were five sons and three daughters in the family. The eldest son, Alvah R., became a physician. He settled in Claremont and practiced his profession there through life, and was long one of the best known physicians in the county. The second son, Ebenezer G., became a dentist, being the first New Hampshire man to graduate from the Philadelphia Dental College. He practiced for a short time in Lancaster, but soon removed to Concord where he soon took, and held through life, first place among the dental practitioners of the city and state. He took a strong interest in public affairs, but never sought nor held office. He was a Democrat in politics, as was his father and elder brother, and a good worker for the party cause.

The second and third sons, George A., and Oscar, engaged in the marble and granite memorial business in Concord, where they continued through life, though Oscar died in early manhood. George A., survived for many years and became prominent in public affairs, having become a Republican and an active partisan, serving in the legislature and as Mayor of the city. He was also prominent in Odd Fellowship, and at one time Master of the Grand Lodge. Milon D., early in life joined his brothers in the marble business in Concord, and there continued till his decease in March last.

Of the three sisters Sally Ann, the eldest, became the wife of Dr. George W. Young of Acworth. Mary Jane, the second, married George A. Young, a Concord dentist, who was also an active Republican politician, the "right hand man" of the late Senator J. H. Gallinger in local affairs, and for some years, preceeding his death, postmaster of Concord. Laura, the youngest daughter, married Elliott Smith, an Acworth farmer, and settled near home where she continued through life.

While speaking of the Cummingses, reference may as well be made here to Major Ephraim Cummings, a brother of Alvah, who was a resident of South Acworth, where he had a fine home and quite a farm, but was particularly interested in music. He was a band master of wide reputation, and not only conducted a band in South Acworth for many years, but also gave instruction to bands and band leaders elsewhere. His son, Charles B. Cummings, who was also quite a musician, operated a peg factory in South Acworth for several years, previous to his decease. George R. Cummings, now a prominent resident of South Acworth, who was instrumental in securing the location of the West Side highway from Bellows Falls through the town, is the son of Charles B.

In the spring of 1860, when I was 19 years of age, my father "gave me my time," as the expression goes. I desired a little more education than I had been able to secure thus far, and as he did not feel able to send me away to school, he gave me this opportunity to earn something for myself, by means of which I might be able to secure some of the schooling that I desired.

I was at loss, for a time, as to how I should employ myself, but finally made a proposition to my father that I carry on the farm on shares. I was to take it, with the stock as it stood, to have one quarter of the year's production, and have the services of my brother, Carlos, next younger, who was then 14 years of age, and also to have my board with the family. I was ambitious and sought to accomplish a great deal, but what I did failed to prove very remunerative. I recall that I raised 600 bushels of potatoes, but the price was low—only a shilling or sixteen and two-thirds cents per bushel, and my quarter, or 150 bushels, amounted to a small sum at that rate, and there was no other selling crop that proved more remunerative. There was an abundance of apples, but no choice fruit, and cider apples, at 10 cents per bushel, added little to my accumulations.

Finding nothing profitable to employ myself

about in the following winter, aside from taking care of the stock, I concluded to attend the district school, more with the idea of fun and recreation than adding to my stock of knowledge. James H. Brown, a younger brother of George R., was the teacher that winter and I think I was the oldest one of the boys in attendance. Among the scholars attending were Milon D., and Laura Cummings, Josephine S. Merrill, daughter of Nathaniel Merrill; Kathleen, Eugene and Ashton E. Hemphill, children of Freeland Hemphill; Grout Campbell, son of Deacon Horace Campbell, Spofford and Carlos Grout, sons of Ebenezer Grout, and Parthenia, daughter of Joseph Gleason. All the men named as parents were substantial farmers and prominent citizens of the town. Freeland Hemphill was a man of great natural ability, well posted in political matters, and an intense Republican, with whom I had more controversy than any other man whom I had known. I should have said all these men except Joseph Gleason were farmers. He had a small farm, exceedingly well tilled, but depended mainly upon his trade as a shoemaker.

All the scholars I have mentioned and all others attending that term of school, have passed away so far as I know, except Spofford and Carlos Grout, who, as I have recently learned, are still living on the Pacific Coast, and Ashton E. Hemphill, a Holyoke, Mass., pharmacist. The last to go, and the last of her generation among the residents on the hill, was Josephine S. Merrill, widow of the late Manley Gassett, a Civil War veteran, who occupied the head seat on the girls' side of the school room during that term of school, as I did that on the boys' side.

Acworth has furnished many men who have been prominent in the public, professional and business life of the country. Urban A. Woodbury, a native of the town, who removed to Vermont, became Governor of that state. Nedom Angier, another native, who was a physician by profession, located in Georgia, and became prominent in public affairs in the "Reconstruction" period, holding the office of state treasurer. Among other physicians, going out from Acworth, aside from Dr. Angier, and Dr. Alvah R. Cummings, previously mentioned, were Dr. Milton Parker, who became eminent in Chicago; Dr. Jonathan Silsby at Cazenovia, N. J., Drs. John H. Hemphill, William Grout and Milton P. Hayward, in Ohio; Dr. Dean W. McKeen, formerly Professor of Therapeutics and Materia Medica in the St. Louis College of Physicians and Surgeons, and later in Kansas; and Drs. N. G. Brooks and Oscar C. Young of Charlestown, N. H.

The legal profession has been well represented by Acworth men. Milon C. McClure, son of Samuel McClure and a graduate of Dartmouth, studied law and practiced in Claremont with much success till his death in 1860, at the early age of 41 years, having served in the state legislature and the Executive Council. Shepard L. Bowers, son of James Bowers, practiced law in Newport from 1856 till his death in 1894. He had been a representative and senator in the legislature, register of probate and county solicitor. Lyman J. and George B. Brooks, sons of Dr. Lyman Brooks, were both lawyers, the former practicing for a time in Claremont, and later serving for several years as Clerk of the Court for Sullivan County, at Newport, and the latter practicing at Saginaw, Mich. George R. Brown, son of Aaron Brown (heretofore mentioned as a teacher) practiced many years in Newport. Adson D. Keyes, son of Adna Keyes, graduate of Dartmouth in the class of 1872, was long in successful practice in Faribault, Minn., and was a lecturer in law in the State University. Herbert D. Ryder, who, though not a native, "grew up" in Acworth, was a prominent lawyer at Bellows Falls, Vt., and prominent in the public life of the state. The ablest lawyer born in the town, however, and one of the ablest in the country, is George W. Anderson, present Associate Justice of the U. S. Circuit Court of Appeals for the First Circuit. He is a son of the late David C. and Martha (Brigham) Anderson, born September 1, 1861, and is a descendant, in the 7th generation, from James Anderson, one of the first 16 settlers of Londonderry, N. H. He is a graduate of Williams College and the Boston University Law School, and commenced practice in Boston in 1900. He is a Democrat and was his party's candidate for Attorney General of the State in 1911 and 1912. He has served as a member of the Boston School Committee, as U. S. District Attorney, as a member of the State Public Service Commission, and was Judge of the U. S. District Court for a time before accepting his present position.

Among Acworth born men prominent in the Christian ministry, was the Rev. Daniel Lancaster, long secretary of the New Hampshire Bible Society. Another was Rev. John Orcutt, D. D., who held pastorates in several different states and was for many years Secretary of the American Colonization Society. Rev. Alexander Houston was another Congregational clergyman, born here, long occupying Maine pastorates; while Rev. Giles Bailey, another native, was a Universalist preacher in the same state. As to recent day clergymen of Acworth origin I have little knowledge, but should not fail to mention Rev. William Prentiss, now holding a Connecticut pastorate, who has been an interesting speaker on more than one Old Home Day occasion in recent years.

In speaking of Acworth's contribution to the medical profession, recently, I failed to mention

Dr. Charles E. Woodbury, a native of the town, now retired, who has had an interesting career. Born in Acworth, November 1, 1845, son of Charles M. and Louise (Graham) Woodbury, graduating from Dartmouth College in 1870 and from the Medical Department of the University of New York in 1873, he served in the N. H. Asylum (now State hospital) as assistant physician for a time, going thence to the McLean Asylum at Waverly, Mass., where he was engaged for several years, and afterwards in the Bloomington, N. Y., Asylum. He was for seven years Superintendent of the R. I. State hospital; was Inspector of Institutions for the Mass. State Board of Lunacy and Charity from 1891 to 1899, and Superintendent of the Foxboro, Mass., state hospital from 1899 to 1908.

Dr. Woodbury was a great lover of music, and a fine singer when in his prime, and when at home in Acworth was of great assistance in the musical services of the church. It may be added that his sister, Helen Louise, was also an accomplished musician, and taught music in the Boston public schools for many years.

It should not be forgotten that Hiram Orcutt, a brother of Rev. John Orcutt, before mentioned, and also an Acworth native, was one of the best known educators in New England. He was a graduate of Dartmouth, of the class of 1842, and was successively the principal of Hebron and

Thetford, Vt., Academies, the Ladies Seminary at North Granville, N. Y., the Glenwood Seminary at Brattleboro, Vt., and Tilden Ladies Seminary at West Lebanon, N. H., which was for some years the most popular girls' school in the state.

William H. Mitchell, born in Acworth, April 10, 1872, a graduate of Dartmouth, class of 1898, has had a successful career as a teacher and is still pursuing the same. He taught in Kenyon Military Academy at Gambier, Ohio, 1899-1906, in the University School at Cleveland, 1906-9, in the Berkshire Hill School at Great Barrington, Mass., and in the Nichols School for boys, at Buffalo, N. Y., where he is now engaged, for many years past.

Mention of Acworth teachers should not be concluded without reference to Myra S. Chatterton. She was educated at Mount Holyoke, and taught successfully in this state and Maryland for several years, but for the last fifteen years before her untimely death in 1907, in a Brooklyn, N. Y., high school, where she won high reputation for competency, as well as the affectionate regard of her scholars, and the esteem of her associates. Her sister, Esther R. Chatterton, who has been a member of the Acworth Board of Education for several years, is the Secretary of the local Old Home Week Association. Another sister, Minnie, has also long been and still is a successful teacher in New York.

Mention has been made of Charles M. Woodbury, father of Dr. Charles E. He was long connected with the old Warner store at the "Town", and was one of the active Democratic leaders, of whom Jonathan H. Dickey (generally known as Harvey) was another. Acworth never had a resident lawyer but Judge Dickey (he held the office of Judge of Probate for a time by appointment by Governor Weston) did a good deal of business as a Justice of the Peace and conveyancer, and his advice was much sought in legal matters. He was a man of high character and universally respected. Other active Democrats of the town were Nathaniel Merrill, Adna Keyes, Charles J. Davis, George Bailey, J. Newton Davis and S. Page Barnard, the latter removing to Minnesota in middle life, with John and Alexander Graham and others.

My first and only political activity in Acworth was during the campaign of 1860, when, although not old enough to be a voter, I espoused the cause of Breckinridge and Lane, and walked to Newport before the election to secure from Hon. Edmund Burke, some of the ballots of that party, of which nine were cast in the town on election day.

The best informed and really the ablest member of the Republican party in the town, was Freeland Hemphill of the Grout Hill district, of whom I have heretofore spoken; but he never engaged in party manipulation, and never sought office. The only office that he ever held, while I lived in the town, was that of prudential committee in the Grout Hill district, and he would accept that only upon condition that one of the young men of the district should go for the school mistress hired for the summer term, and relieve him of that duty. Jesse and Zenas Slader, Daniel J. Warner, William Prentiss, Rodney Buss, James A. Reed, Dr. N. G. Brooks, Chapin K. Brooks and James A. Wood were some of the men who manipulated the wires in the Republican machine. Chapin K. Brooks was particularly active for a time when he was proprietor of the general store of the town. James A. Wood became quite prominent after the older men went off the stage, and came to be regarded as the party "boss" for a number of years.

As has been said, Acworth was regarded as a good farming town; much better than Lempster. The soil was stronger, more fertile and more easily cultivated. While agriculture was the leading industry and many of the farmers thrifty and well to do, there was quite a little manufacturing during the first half or two-thirds of the last century. There were several lumber mills and wood working establishments at different points on Cold River, especially at East Acworth, then known as Buss Hollow or Keyes Hollow, and at Parks Hollow, or South Acworth. At the latter locality there was also a small woolen mill, operated, during the time of my stay in town, by Nathan Adams, who had come into the place from the town of Washington. This mill turned out about 6000 yards of woolen cloth per year at that time, but went to decay and disappeared long ago.

There was also a grist mill at South Acworth, and a shoe peg manufactory, operated by Major Ephraim Cummings and his son, Charles B., and later by the latter alone. It was in this factory that shoe pegs were first made by machinery in this country. Going out of the peg business, later Mr. Cummings was for some time engaged in the manufacture of clothes pins. At the present time no vestige of any of these mills remains.

For a number of years there was quite a business in the manufacture of boots and shoes carried on in Acworth. The Acworth Boot & Shoe Co., so-called, had a factory at the "Town", near the Warner store, where considerable business was done for a number of years and another establishment of the kind was located at a little settlement, about a mile south east of the village, which came to be known by the name of "Lynn", on account of this business.

The decadence of this fine old hill town is strikingly indicated in the decline in population from 1523 in 1810 to about 500 at the present time. This decline is no greater than in many towns of the state, but the conditions here are more favorable to agricultural success than in most other towns that show the same measure of falling off, on account of the superior quality of the land. It is not too much to hope that ere the present century is completed the "back to the farm" tide, already setting in, in some sections, will reach Acworth, and thrift and prosperity again be manifest upon the old farms that cover its sunny hillsides.

In the spring of 1861, accompanied by George R. Brown, I went to Swanzey, N. H., where Burrill Porter, Jr., a native of the town of Langdon, and an experienced teacher was acting as principal of the old school known as Mt. Caesar Seminary. Mr. Brown and I boarded with the principal's family, paying the sum of two dollars per week for board and laundry service. Somewhat late in life he had determined to go to college, and was preparing for the same, while, though studying Latin and Greek, I had no such purpose, but was seeking such mental discipline as such schooling as I could afford would furnish.

At the completion of the spring term, I returned to Acworth and passed the summer at farm work, a part of the time on the home place, and a part elsewhere; but in the fall went, again to Swanzey to the same school as in the spring, which maintained but two terms in the year at this period of its existence. For this term I was accompanied not only by Mr. Brown, but also by several others, including my brother, Carl, and Nathaniel P. Merrill. A young man from Keene, named William Hartwell, also joined our party, and the five of us, together, hired a tenement, paying $3 per month for the same and set up housekeeping for ourselves, cooking our own food, such as we did not buy already prepared in Keene, five miles distant, to which place some of us, or all together, walked at least once a week. At the close of the term we found that it had cost us, just $1.06 apiece a week. The term was a fairly profitable one all around. We all learned something at least, and made some very pleasant acquaintances. One which I have always cherished was that with George W. Gay of Swanzey, a student in my class in Latin, who subsequently became a distinguished Boston physician and surgeon. His two sisters, Ella and Annie, also attended the school, with whom I have maintained a pleasant acquaintance, though the latter passed away a few months since.

There was no regular term of the school in the winter, but Mr. Porter taught the village district school; and Mr. Brown and myself remained through the winter, keeping the tenement that we had hired in the fall, and boarding ourselves as before and reciting to Mr. Porter in the evenings.

Returning home in the spring, I engaged to

work on a farm till fall, for one Reuben Angier, who subsequently removed to Newport, for the munificent sum of $15 per month. I had a laborious time of it, but got through all right, and early in October, accompanied by Nathaniel P. Merrill, started for Michigan, our objective being the Law Department of the University at Ann Arbor, after earning enough to give us the necessary start. When we landed in Detroit it was a straggling city of 70,000 inhabitants. Today its population far exceeds 1,000,000; but I do not claim that our arrival or departure had any effect upon its growth, which was, indeed, not particularly marked till Henry Ford came along a good deal later.

We went to Oakland County, about 25 miles from Detroit, where I had some relatives; taught district schools in the winter; did farm work the next spring and summer, and in the following autumn—that of 1863, entered as students in the Law Department of the University, as we had originally planned, paying an entrance or tuition fee of $10 each. We hired two rooms in the fourth story of a Main Street block, and boarded ourselves, as at Swanzey. There were about 80 students in our class, but I can say, without boasting that none made a better showing in studies and examination than we two, who were the first New Hampshire men to graduate from that department, which we did in the spring of 1865.

When we left Ann Arbor, that spring, Merrill went west to Iowa, but I returned home to New Hampshire, in poor health, and afflicted with a hard cough, from which I was not relieved for several months. My father had sold his Grout Hill farm to Deacon George W. Young, and removed across the river, to a smaller farm, previously owned by Leavitt McKeen, just above the Aaron Brown place, where I spent most of the time, recuperating in health, keeping at the farm work to some extent and performing such odd jobs as came to hand. Having regained my strength in a measure, I cut a lot of pulp wood for James H. Brown, who had charge of his father's farm, in the winter, and assisted him in the maple orchard in the spring, one of our operations being the building of a new sugar house.

Speaking of the Browns, some mention of the family may be in order. Aaron and Eadey (Watts) Brown, who lived on this large rough and rocky, but fairly productive farm, now owned, and occupied in the summer, with much adjoining land, by True Tucker, son of B. Frank Tucker of Concord, who married Emma Watts of Acworth, a cousin of the Brown children, who by the way was doing house work for the family that winter, had four sons and three daughters. The eldest son, Isaac, emigrated to Indiana in early manhood, where he engaged in farming and continued through life. John, the second son located in Walpole, where he also was a successful farmer and prominent citizen, representing the town in the legislature, and holding various other offices. George R. and James H., the other sons have already been mentioned. Diana, the eldest daughter, married one George Lewis of Marlow, and subsequently removed with him to Claremont. Melissa was the wife of Samuel Savory of Alstead, and Maria, the youngest, married one Moses Moulton, who lived for a time in Alstead but finally removed to Manchester.

During the winter of 1865-6, a term of the old Lyceum was held at South Acworth, which I very naturally attended though many of those who had participated in the exercises in the previous years of my attendance were there no more. New members, however, had come in and the sessions were generally interesting. One of the men specially active in the debates was Elisha M. Kempton, now the "grand old man" of Newport at 95 years of age, who, with his father, was then residing on a farm, some two miles up the river from the village, near the junction of the Marlow road with the main line. Mr. Kempton was a strong and interesting speaker, well informed upon the subjects under discussion and always attentively listened to. Another new speaker was Adson D., or Dean

Keyes, as he was usually called. His father, Adna Keyes, had recently moved into South Acworth village, from his farm in the east part of the town, near Buss Hollow, and built a fine residence. His daughter, Jennie, a handsome girl and fine musician, also added much to the interest of the Lyceum, in the miscellaneous programs. She subsequently removed to California, where she was the wife of a man named Merriam, and is now residing at Venice, not far from Los Angeles in that state. Another young woman, who contributed much to the literary work of the Lyceum, was a Miss Emma Nelson, who taught a select school there in the fall, and was the teacher of the district school in the winter. Among the younger people taking part in the Lyceum exercises were Charles A. Brackett, whose family had moved into Acworth from Lempster, and to whom I have previously referred as a noted dentist, and Ellen Atwood of Alstead, who became Mrs. W. P. Chamberlain of Keene. I have a very distinct recollection of these two as "Snarley" and "Grumpy" in the play of "The Quiet Family", put on by the Lyceum, at one time during the winter, in which I took the part of Benjamin Bibbs; while my brother Carl enacted that of Barnaby Bibbs.

In the spring of 1866 I went to Newport and entered the office of Hon. Edmund Burke, making my home in his family and paying my way by caring for his garden and ten acres of land which he owned a mile up on the road toward Croydon. I have already spoken of my experience in this connection, and of my admission to the bar in September, 1866. One of the interesting incidents of my life in Newport that year was my connection with the Lyceum there, which had been revived for the fall season, and in which some of the lawyers participated, as well as the law students, Howard, Collester and myself. One of the men, who took an active part in the discussions, was the Rev. Paul S. Adams, a retired Baptist clergyman, whose young daughter, then about a dozen years of age, subsequently became the wife of George W. Britton, who removed to Concord and there engaged in the hardware trade now carried on by his son, Arthur H. Britton, chairman of the Merrimack County Board of Commissioners and Vice President of the Universalist State Convention.

Among the young ladies contributing helpfully to the literary work of the Lyceum was Miss Etta Guild, a native of Walpole, then a clerk in the Newport postoffice, who was not only a bright writer but also a fine musician. She subsequently married Capt. Richard Musgrove of Bristol, and is the mother of Ex-Speaker Frank A. Musgrove, Miss Mary Musgrove of the Bristol Enterprise, and other notable members of what was for a time known as the "Musgrove Family", concert musicians.

I continued my studies in Mr. Burke's office through the fall of 1866, but left in the early winter to replenish my funds by canvassing for Lunt's "Origin of the War" which work I followed with varied success, in different parts of the state, for some months. George R. Brown, whom I have heretofore mentioned more than once, who had graduated from Tufts in the previous summer, took my place as a student in Mr. Burke's office, and in his home.

During my stay in Newport I made comparatively few acquaintainces and my social calls were limited to few families. At the homes of Matthew Harvey, whose wife had been one of my early teachers, and who had two attractive daughters—Sophia and Minnie—of William Dunton, whose wife was Lois Corbin, a daughter of Austin Corbin, Sr., and a woman of rare intelligence whose friendship I valued highly as well as that of her daughter, Mary, and of Rev. Thompson Barron, with several grown daughters, the elder of whom, Emroy, was an accomplished musician and a very bright woman (afterwards Mrs. John M. Shirley of Andover) I was a frequent visitor. All of these people, so far as I know, have passed "over the river," as well as most of the men who were then active in the public and business life of the town. One of the latter whom I pleasantly recall, was E. C. Converse, prominent druggist and active Democrat, who was for some time moderator at the town meetings when the Democrats were in the ascendant, as was not infrequently the case in those days.

Although not at home at the time, I was chosen a delegate to the State Convention of the party by the Democrats of Acworth in January, 1867, my colleague from that town being Adna Keyes. I had been canvassing in the lower part of the State, and went to Concord for "the night before", putting up at the old Columbian Hotel, then managed by that loyal Democrat, Joseph H. Mace. It so happened that Mr. Burke was made president of the State Convention, and his address on taking the chair was pointed and telling.

This convention, by the way, unanimously nominated Hon. John G. Sinclair of Bethlehem for Governor, and instructed him to challenge Gen. Walter Harriman, the Republican candidate to a joint debate in the campaign, throughout the state, which he proceeded to do, and the debate that followed was one of the most interesting and exciting ever held in this or any other state, as some men now living may remember. Gen. Harriman was elected by a vote of 35,809 to 32,663 for Mr. Sinclair, but not on the merits of the debate, as it was generally conceded that Sinclair was the more effective speaker.

The delegates from Newport in this convention

were Edmund Burke, Edmund Wheeler, H. A. Averill and C. T. Lathrop; while Unity sent Ransom Severns and Ora M. Huntoon; Lempster, Nathan George and Hiram Parker and Sunapee, William C. Sturoc and Daniel A. George. Hosea W. Parker was one of the delegation of six from Claremont. It may be of interest to add that Newport's representatives in the Legislature that year were H. A. Averill and Charles Emerson, while Unity sent Ransom Severns, Lempster Nathan George, Acworth William Hayward; Sunapee, William C. Sturoc and Goshen William H. McCrillis, father of John McCrillis, present Clerk of the Sullivan County Court. None of these men are now living and no others who were delegates from Sullivan County, or who served in the Legislature from the county that year, when Levi W. Barton of Newport represented the Tenth District in the State Senate.

In June, 1867, I went with Chester E. Carey, a Lempster boy, who had learned the printer's trade and was then employed on the Lyndon, Vt., Union, to the town of Littleton, in Grafton County, in which no Democratic paper was then published, and only one Republican paper—the Free Press at Lebanon, by the late Elias H. Cheney, to look over the ground with reference to the publication of a Democratic paper. The outlook seemed promising and the result was the purchase of a small independent paper called the

Gazette, then published there, and its plant, to which material additions were made, and the subsequent establishment of the White Mountain Republic, vigorously Democratic, with Carey as publisher and myself as editor. At the time I purposed, ultimately to go farther north and engage in the practice of law for which I had fitted myself, but the fascination of journalism, and my devotion to Democratic principles, which as an editor I have ever supported to the extent of my ability, were so strong that such purpose was not carried out, and I continued my newspaper work, in different places and under varied conditions, for most of my life, the circumstances of which have no relation to Sullivan County or these Recollections thereof.

In these "Recollections" I have referred mainly to Men and Matters in those towns of Sullivan County in which I resided and with whom and which I was personally familiar, incidentally alluding to some other towns to which my knowledge and acquaintance extended. I have made little reference to the large and enterprising town of Claremont, which I seldom visited in my boyhood and then only in attendance upon County fairs, and since only on public occasions, like religious conventions, Grange gatherings, or Board of Trade meetings, though I distinctly recall my first visit there, when I went with my father when I was about seven years of age, and he was making a payment on the mortgage held by the late George B. Upham upon the East Unity farm when my father had purchased it. Said Upham, who was a lawyer and former Congressman, was a man of great wealth for that time, and had mortgages upon many farms all over the county. He was the richest man in Sullivan County at the time of his death and his estate inventoried over $400,000.

I may properly add, however, that on one comparatively recent occasion I was a Claremont visitor. This was when in the fall of 1914, I attended the celebration of the town's 150th anniversary celebration, when, as State Historian, no Claremont resident or native having been found available, I gave the historical address.

Of Charlestown, old "Number Four", a strategic point in old Indian war times, I knew little except that it was the home of eminent lawyers, such as John J. Gilchrist, subsequently Chief Justice of the Court of Claims at Washington, D. C., Edmund L. Cushing, long president of the Sullivan County Bar, and later Chief Justice of the Supreme Court of the State, and Henry Hubbard, Ex-Gvoernor and United States Senator, as well as once Speaker pro-tem of the U. S. House of Representatives. Langdon I had never visited in my youth, and knew of it only as the home of Robert Elwell, noted agriculturist and president of the N. H. Agricultural Society, whose fine cattle won many premiums at the state fairs, and as the birthplace of Burrill Porter, Jr., one of New Hampshire's best teachers.

Plainfield, I knew nothing about, except that it was a great sheep town and that Kimball Union Academy was located in its principal village. In later days I knew a Plainfield man named Daniel C. Westgate, who was prominent in Grange circles and for a time a member of the Board of Agriculture for Sullivan County. In political life I had met William C. True and Converse Cole of Meriden, both active Democrats and prominent business men, and in the fall of 1910 I went to Plainfield to make a political speech, being then a candidate for Congress on the Democratic ticket. I stopped over night with a clergyman named McCartney, who was a Democratic candidate for representative in the Legislature, and our meeting was down at "The Plain". I remember more about attending the chapel exercises at the Academy, the next morning, than I do about the political rally.

As for Grantham, I never saw the town until recently, though I knew it was the "stamping ground" of Oliver B. Buswell, a Democratic "war horse" of the early days, and that my friend, Dr. Willard O. Hurd practiced there many years; also that it was the birthplace and summer home of Edwin G. Eastman, Exeter lawyer and some time Attorney General of the State, whom I knew well for many years.

Springfield was also little known to me, but two of its best known citizens I knew well—Charles McDaniel and Dr. George P. Goodhue. Mr. McDaniel was for a time Master of the State Grange, Chairman of the State Board of Agriculture, later of the Board of Equalization, and a Democratic candidate for Congress.

Sunapee I knew as the home of William C. Sturoc, and a charming lake resort, where at the "Ben Mere Inn", in later days, as Secretary of the State Board of Trade I worked off a speaking programme, at an outing of the Board, with the late Wilbur H. Powers of Boston and Croydon, and a young man named Ernest M. Hopkins, a native of Dunbarton, then in business in Boston, as the speakers. Said Hopkins has since been heard of more effectively. I might add that while a resident of Manchester, and later, I knew a prominent native of Sunapee in the person of Gen. Charles H. Bartlett, lawyer and politician and Clerk of the U. S. Court; whose nephew, John H., whom I have since known also, a native of the town has cut quite a figure in the political arena in recent time.

Of Washington I have known little, except that I canvassed it once for a Democratic newspaper and later there attended a Grange anniversary; attended school in my early youth with a Washington young lady as teacher, as I have heretofore noted, and was present at the town's 150th anniversary celebration last August.

Sullivan County is small in territory and its population is correspondingly limited; but in its agricultural and manufacturing interests, and the possibilities of progress therein, as well as in the beauty and variety of its scenery and the healthfulness of its climate, it compares favorably with other counties or sections of the state, or of any state. Out from its borders have gone in the past men and women who have done splendid work in all fields of activity; while those that have remained at home have proved worthy descendants of a noble ancestry.

In the coming year the county will have completed a hundred years of corporate existence. The century mark should be noted by fitting observance.

HENRY H. METCALF

HENRY H. METCALF

www.ingramcontent.com/pod-product-compliance
Lightning Source LLC
Chambersburg PA
CBHW071442160426
43195CB00013B/2002